# GODSWAY

## My Anecdotes with God

Diana Skidmore Keathley

For information, contact

MSI Press, LLC

1760-F Airline Hwy #203

Hollister, CA 95023

Copyeditor: Betty Lou Leaver

Cover design & layout: Opeyemi Ikuborije

ISBN: 978-1-957354-30-9

Library of Congress Control Number: 2023903520

# CONTENTS

# Acknowledgments

The completion of this project would have been impossible without the help of many people who participated directly in it and those who supported and cheered the work on.

My heart-felt gratitude goes to my loving husband, Nowlin, whose patience with my long hours at the computer demonstrates his conviction to partner with me and the Spirit in bringing these true stories to the world. His encouragement and all-in attitude, even in the process of recovering years of work from a damaged flash drive which threatened to halt everything in its track, have meant more to me than I could ever express. His gentle scoldings after many too-long stationary sessions of staring at a screen have no doubt also helped save my vision and my knees.

I sincerely appreciate my children and extended family members for their help in establishing timelines and sequences of events in retrospect, for their encouraging responses after reading various individual chapters, and also for their patience with my absenteeism in many of the daily routines while I was writing.

I am deeply grateful to the friends, acquaintances, and family members who play supporting roles in the stories and who have granted their permission for the authentic retelling of these events.

I cannot adequately express my profound gratitude for the exemplary work of the entire MSI Press, LLC staff, and especially for my editor, Betty Lou Leaver, who has patiently answered the dozens of my novice questions and who is the guiding force in my transition from writer to author-partner in the world of book publishing. From the moment I hit

Send on the initial query email, I have found in her not only a mentor but a true kindred spirit.

Last, but certainly most important, I am eternally grateful to God Almighty, whose right hand has held me and guided me through a lifetime of extraordinary experiences. It is a profound and humbling privilege to witness the love, power, and goodness of God to such a magnitude and at such close range. May the publishing of these Divine encounters be to His eternal glory and to the increased faith of His people.

# Introduction
## Daddy's Girl

Did you ever think about jumping off a building? No, I don't mean in a suicidal way. If that's what you're thinking, you should call a crisis helpline immediately, seek professional guidance, and then finish reading this book. What I mean is, have you ever thought about the circumstances in which you would consider doing something so irrational, illogical, and yes, dangerous, that you would never do it under normal conditions?

Like stuntmen in a movie, you'd want to know there was something there to catch you, say a net. And you'd have to trust the people on the ground enough to be assured they would hold on to the net tightly, not to let you hit the ground, right? It would help to know they'd had lots of practice and had successfully held the net for other jumpers. And you'd probably want to talk first-hand to those guys, or at least read up on what their experiences were like.

At this point, you're probably saying to yourself, "No, I'd just go back inside and take the elevator or stairs down to the first floor." Yeah, that would be much easier and safer. But what if the building were on fire, the elevator jammed, and the stairwell impassable from thick smoke? When the usual safe predictable modes of exit are not an option, then what?

Even if the well trained and experienced fire fighters on the ground were yelling at you, commanding you to jump, it would still be hard to get past your fear and actually fling yourself off the edge, right? Remember when you were a kid and your Dad coaxed you into jumping off the side of

3

the pool, into his waiting arms there in the water? Even that was hard – at least the first time. But off a building? Well maybe, if the fire fighter was your Dad, and you were five.

But what if the building is starting to collapse and the flames are at your back? I can pretty much guarantee the immediate threat of the buckling walls will outweigh your fear of what *might* happen if you jump. You'll obey the fire fighter's command and take the leap—even if he's not your dad. It will be out of desperation, because there is no other choice. But once you're safely on the ground, you realize that if you ever have to do it again you won't even hesitate the next time. It will be a leap of faith. You'll trust the net holders, based on a real past outcome.

That's the situation I was in on the highway in a spinning, bouncing automobile when my Father commanded me to, well, not exactly jump. Since the analogy is breaking down and I'm getting way ahead of myself, let's put it in perspective and start from the beginning...

I was a classic example of a "Daddy's girl." When my brother Kenny came along just 11 months behind me, I was still a baby myself. My dad used to joke, when people would ask if we were twins, that we were "twins on the installment plan."

During the daytime, when Dad was at work, my mother learned to juggle Kenny and me from high chair to playpen to naptime all on her own, while also taking care of my two older sisters, who were still very young. There are even reports Mom was seen more than once with me cradled in one arm and Kenny in the other, feeding me spoonsful of baby food while giving him a bottle simultaneously. Even before multitasking was a word, she was definitely a super mom!

In the evenings and on weekends, however, while Mom was busy with the newest addition—and the rest of the household, Dad took me under his wing. At mealtime, he cut my food and fed me, smashing my baked potatoes to a perfect paste of half butter and half potato. He would fly the airplane into the hangar, a metaphor from his war years, to get the green beans down me.

Though he didn't talk about the war much when we were growing up, war references were always in the background. He would playfully "circle for the landing" and finally "set her down easy" while feeding Kenny or me. I thought it was such a grand game! Even as a pretty big kid of four years old I would plead with him at dinnertime, after he had cut up my meat, "Daddy, feed me, feed me! " On other occasions, when we misbehaved, his scolding glare was always in tandem with the war-era admonition to "straighten up and fly right!"

From as early as the feedings in the high chair, I was fascinated with his references to flying. My eyes followed the swirling spoon through the air and to my mouth long before I understood the actual words he was saying.

Dad's favorite poem was "High Flight," written by a young Canadian pilot, John Gillespie Magee Jr., not long before he crashed and died early in the war. Dad used to quote lines from the poem, to my great pleasure,

> Oh! I have slipped the surly bonds of Earth
> And danced the skies on laughter-silvered wings;
> Sunward I've climbed and joined the tumbling mirth
> Of sun-split clouds—and done a hundred things
> You have not dreamed of...

These images and sensations described by the poet had struck a chord with Dad because he'd experienced them with an equal exuberance. He laughed with delight telling my uncles about doing barrel rolls and stalls with the new recruits. Just at the point when the nose of the plane comes down out of a stall and they'd start into the dive, he'd watch with amusement as some of the recruits got sick and others "had the stomach for it." He truly loved flying, at least the thrill of it.

In his older years, once in a while Dad would open up and share other kinds of experiences from the war. I know now they were life-changing for him. He told us about when he was a flight instructor in India and China, responsible for training groups of young pilots to take off and land within a very specific short and narrow space. They had to be so exact. So precise in their judgements and actions. He would mark off the distance on the field to represent the space on an aircraft carrier within which they would have to maneuver. He wanted to drill it in during practice so it would be second nature when the new pilots actually had to make those difficult takeoffs and landings when it counted in combat.

He spoke with reverence and would tear up 50 years later telling of an incident in which one young man, whose name I don't remember but he recalled instantly while recounting the tragedy, didn't quite get it right. The young would-be pilot crashed into the runway while Dad and others looked on. The weight of responsibility fell heavily on him to make sure he did everything he possibly could to train them well, and the loss was personal.

He told of another time when he was on a patrol mission, not in a battle but looking for enemy presence in the area. The small squadron finished their rounds and headed back to the base when for some reason Dad decided to make one more pass. He came out of a thick cloud into a small clear patch only to see an enemy plane directly in front of him. They were so close he could see the Japanese pilot's face, and their eyes locked in that instant when they both reacted and peeled off to avoid a crash.

It was a split-second reaction on both their parts. Only later did Dad fully admit how close a call it had been. Pondering the significance of that encounter, he had seen, instead of an enemy, a sort of reflection of himself. I think in powerful, quiet moments as a pilot, Dad shared another experience with the young poet: he did indeed discover personally and reach out to touch the face of God.

But I knew little of those things when I was young. I had no idea what war was or what my father had accomplished as a fighter pilot and a flight instructor in the past. I only knew that from the moment I was born, he was my home-front hero.

In addition to feeding me at dinner, he helped me with dozens of routine daily tasks. He put my socks on me, twisting the heel and toe sections to fit perfectly. He patiently found the tiny holes in the ankle straps that buckled my white patent leather sandals. He brushed my hair, and on hair-washing days, he painstakingly combed the tangles out, always working from the bottom up. On a few occasions he tried his hand at making my pin curls, though they were never as secure as when Mom did them.

He even trimmed my bangs once as an unsolicited favor to my mother. However, they turned out so uneven after whacking the whole handful of hair in one long sawing motion that he continued to trim in a persevering effort to get the buggers straight. Ultimately, where too-long bangs had been, only an inch of fringe remained, far above my eyebrows. Needless to say, he only did that little chore the one time!

On weekdays, late in the afternoon I sensed when it was time to start listening for the sound of the Ford Fairlane pulling into the driveway. Sometimes Dad would stop at the grocery store to pick up a few things we needed before the weekend shopping. If he was much later than I thought he should be, I would fret and hound Mom every minute or two with my insistent question, "When is Daddy going to be home?!"

Finally, I would hear the car outside the window and race to hide behind the front door. I wanted to jump out and "scare" him as he came in. Many a time, Dad stumbled through the living room with a grocery sack in each arm. With me hanging for dear life onto his leg, he was trying not to step on me and fumbling to keep his balance long enough to set the groceries on the dining room table. Then, he'd scoop me up and give me a bear hug. The best part of my day was just beginning.

He used to wrestle and play with us kids in the floor. Ham that he was, he'd feign injury, telling my older sisters or Ken, "Oh, you broke my leg!" or "Whew! You're too strong for me. Uncle! Uncle!" Well, being the daddy's girl that I was, I thought it was my job to take care of him as much as it was his to take care of me. I would shout "Don't you hurt my daddy!" and lay into the others with both arms flailing so fast that Dad would get tickled at my "windmill treatment." He'd have to fess up and call the game off so that no one would really get hurt.

To keep the noise and bickering to a minimum on long car trips—a staple with four young children in such tight quarters—Dad would invariably start singing. Mom would soon chime in since she knew every word to the favorite songs of the period. I was enchanted from the beginning to hear them sing together. When Dad would forget the words, he'd let Mom continue in the lead, and he would start humming a harmony part. My first favorite songs were theirs—memorable tunes from their youth and the post-war era like "Shine On, Harvest Moon" and "Young at Heart."

I remember vividly the time I asked Dad to teach me to sing harmony. As he taught me to find the third note and listen for chord combinations in a certain key, I cut my teeth on classics like "Church in the Wildwood," "Down by the Old Mill Stream," and Mom's favorite hymns like "Love Lifted Me" and "Ivory Tower."

Dad was creative in the ways he countered our sibling rivalries and inevitable squabbling. He taught us a silly game in which two people would face off, one the kitty and the other its owner. The kitty was to meow, act distressed, and try to make the owner laugh. The owner was to pet the kitty on the head and say "poor kitty" three times without laughing or cracking a smile. We would giggle immediately at Dad's goofy faces and silly antics when he played the kitty, but there was rarely so much as a hint of a grin when he was the owner.

In fact, in an instant, in the middle of a belly laugh at something, he could draw a hand down his face from his forehead to his chin and reveal a calm unsmiling demeanor on the other side and maintain it. His restraint was remarkable to me even as a child.

I practiced not allowing myself to laugh, along with more and more outlandish versions of a meow and increasingly exaggerated facial expressions as the kitty. Eventually, I mastered the arts both of soliciting laughter and of stoic composure and won every game with my siblings and friends.

Those 'skills' came in handy repeatedly later. When I needed to avoid would-be ticklers, Dad would respond to my complaints with "Just pretend it doesn't tickle, and they'll leave you alone." I followed his advice and endured the tickling for a minute or two without giving in to laughter and found he was right. My older cousins left me alone after that. I'd taken the fun out of it for them.

Years later, as a teacher, it was easy to connect with students when I could laugh with them, even at myself, to put them at ease. Or I could put on my stern 'teacher face' in an instant when the occasion called for it.

On Sundays, Dad would brush out the dried pin curls, fold my lace anklets down perfectly, and tie the big bow just right in the back of my dress to go to Sunday school and church. He wasn't going with us, which bothered me immensely at the time. I didn't understand until many years later why. He was the epitome of love, strength, wisdom, and safety for me. He knew everything and could do no wrong, well, except the bangs. Those were blissfully happy early years.

Then, sometime when I was 4-5 years old, I started having horrible episodes of fear. I think they began shortly after Uncle Oscar died. My Grandma Harney's oldest brother was scary enough when he was alive: old and scraggly-looking, with long yellow fingernails. He had false teeth that he would thrust out suddenly at us kids for the sole purpose of hearing us squeal. He would laugh gleefully at his success and then wiggle his bony tobacco-stained fingers, making the eerie "Wooooo" noise to get another rise out of us. Being so young, I didn't understand his odd sense of humor; those were not particularly good experiences with him.

Then suddenly, there he was lying all stiff and waxy-looking in an open casket in Grandma's living room. Everyone was sad and crying. I didn't know what to think of it all, and it raised so many questions—questions I would struggle for years to find answers to.

The fear came on unexpectedly after that, at the mere mention of illness, death, heaven, hell, eternity. My thoughts would spiral out of control and waves of sheer terror would wash over me. I never knew when it would hit me.

One such occasion was triggered by a turtle expiring in the science room at McKinley Elementary School. I believe I was in second grade. I cried through the whole class period though the teacher tried to comfort me with thoughts of heaven, comparing its beauty with the rainbow-like colors on the inside of the turtle shell. Her words were prophetic, but it was not comforting at the time to think of living in a shell forever, no matter how pretty it was.

I was upset all day at school and inconsolable by the time Dad got home from work. I climbed in his lap and asked him to tell me about heaven. People always pointed up toward heaven, and my childish mind couldn't imagine much beyond some sort of giant attic in the sky. What would it be like? How would it look? Would we be able to walk around? Would we all be together? Would there be *room* for everyone? That was a genuine concern for me since I had a very large and loving extended family on both my mom's and dad's side, whom I wanted to be included. I had so many questions.

That night was my first realization that my Daddy didn't know everything. He didn't have all the answers I needed. At least, he was honest with me. I never thought until years later about how hard it must have been for him to look into his daughter's adoring, searching eyes and say those words so void of comfort, "I don't know, honey." He didn't try to make anything up. He was quiet for several minutes before he went on. "I don't know what heaven will be like, but if God can make mountains and trees, I'm sure heaven will be beautiful." His answer seemed inadequate, at best, for me, and I suspect now, for him, too.

Dad didn't talk a lot about God, and for many years I wondered why he didn't go to church with us. I only learned as an adult that he was very much turned off by the hypocrisy he saw in so many of the church-going people he knew as a boy and young man, but that doesn't mean he wasn't a man of faith. He definitely was, but it was an inner faith between him and God only.

Most likely he grew into his faith gradually through each new phase of his life. Born in Oologah, Oklahoma, he grew up with a strict father, who periodically worked out of town for a week or more at a time during the Great Depression. He had adult expectations of my dad and his brothers, all mere boys, as he instructed them to tend gardens and orchards in his absence as he would have or face the strap.

Later, Dad flunked out of freshman year at university. Class clown and straight-A-student was not a combination he could pull off beyond his small high school. It was an embarrassment to him, and he thought to his family, also. He made up for it by attending the nearby military academy in Claremore instead and went on to flying school through the FDR work program. He later faced firsthand the traumas of war and combat.

With all he had been through, Dad knew better than most that his relationship with God was deeply personal and that he was answerable only to God Himself and not to what other people assumed about him.

It used to frustrate me when various people in the family would try to talk to him about his "need to accept Christ," go to church, be baptized, or whatever thing it was they thought he had to do to be saved. But he knew all along it was more than just walking down an aisle, saying a specific prayer, or doing any of the things people thought he should do.

Yet, he never reacted negatively, at least to my knowledge, toward those who were proselytizing. He listened respectfully and never argued theological points nor got into any robust debates, knowing they spoke out of love for him. If he replied at all, I suspect it was similar to the response he gave me when, after a few such occasions I was aware of when I was older, I would feel so defensive on his behalf. We would talk, and he would defend the person, saying that she (it was usually one of my aunts) was only doing what she thought was right. He would assure me with a smile, "I am at peace with my Maker."

He was. He told me once he had read the Bible through from cover to cover, and though he didn't pretend to understand all of it, he did his best to actually live his faith instead of just talk about it.

Growing up during the Great Depression and being involved in World War II, Dad had seen a lot of suffering and poverty. He had gotten to know people who had very few material possessions but who shared a sense of right and wrong and a sense of common humanity. After seeing immense deprivation overseas, he came home with a new appreciation for the bounty we live in here in the United States, and he was not going to let us kids take it for granted.

We were taught to be good stewards of everything we had: food, water, allowance money, everything. We ate every bite we put on our plate and learned the hard way not to let our eyes be bigger than our stomachs. We were dogged about turning off the water faucet completely and firmly to avoid dripping and were programmed to always turn the lights off when leaving a room not to waste electricity. We were coached to use only a few squares of toilet paper and fold them neatly, rather than yanking off long spinning streams to wad up. We were trained to put the lid back on everything, and we learned the art of squeezing the last molecule of toothpaste out of the tube.

He didn't do this because we were poor and couldn't afford another roll of toilet paper or tube of toothpaste but precisely because we had so much while others in the world had so little. It was our obligation to be frugal and thankful for all of it.

It is difficult to overstate the profound influence Dad had in shaping my perspectives and attitudes about character, family, and other people as well as about life and the world in general. It was so much more than him being my primary care giver during my first years. His lasting effect on me had as much to do with the man he was, as with being my Daddy. He wasn't perfect by any means, but I always knew he was a great man, a wise man, a man of integrity, and a man full of love and compassion.

He taught us to be honest, to be truthful, to say what we mean and mean what we say, to understand that a person's word is a trustworthy promise that can be counted on, and to be careful with our words. (Not that we always listened!) He cautioned us not to judge people until we had "walked a mile in their shoes." He encouraged us to put ourselves in other people's situations and try to imagine how they felt and how we might have acted in the same circumstance.

He was a good father, and true to his teaching, he kept his word. When he made a promise, he did everything within his human power to keep it, no matter how difficult, inconvenient, or uncomfortable it might become to do so.

I remember one summer when he had promised we would go to the drive-in movie the following Saturday. On the appointed day, an unexpected late afternoon thunderstorm brought up the question as to whether we should cancel our plans and go another time. But prompted by my insistence, "Daddy, you promised!" he kept his word, and we went. We could hardly see the screen for the rain, and we couldn't close the window tightly enough around the speaker hung on it to keep the spray from coming in. But a promise was a promise.

Equally, there was no changing his mind about any other decision he had made concerning us kids, no hope of any wiggle room. If he said we were *not* going somewhere, he was *not* buying us something, or we were *not* spending the night with our cousin Amelia, there was no amount of begging, pleading, or case building that could budge his resolve. At least not to the point of showing outwardly or changing his mind.

I guess he thought it would be seen as ambivalence or weakness. The military had taught him you couldn't be a good leader if you were indecisive or wishy-washy. You had to judge the situation and make the best decision you could make based on the information you had. Then, stick to it!

So, being this Daddy's girl, I learned, especially in my teenage and college years, to build my case toward any decision I wanted. I would anticipate and answer all the possible questions. I'd counter all the likely objections or negative reactions he might have before I ever asked for his permission because once the verdict was rendered, there was no further appeal to be made.

It wasn't until much later in his life that he conceded it was okay to change his mind or opinion about something based on new evidence or as he grew in understanding. He loved to read and learn new things. He was fascinated by new discoveries in the realms of science, archeology, and outer space. He noticed when many of the "new" discoveries confirmed things he had been taught as a child from the "old, old story" about God and the Bible.

We saw him soften in the latter years. The stoic glare that we thought was going to ignite our eyeballs when we were in trouble as kids gave way to watery eyes at stories of human kindness and self-sacrifice. He was touched and humbled by them. The growth of his inward faith, perspective, and understanding was part of his life's journey. To the end it was, though never perfect on the human front, a life well-lived, full of love, integrity, humility, gratitude, and an overwhelming sense of being blessed far beyond what he deserved. He certainly paid it forward to me, and to everyone who knew him.

GODSWAY

# Earliest Encounters

Like my Dad's, my spiritual journey did not begin with a typical "conversion" experience. I could never point to any one moment when I "accepted Christ" or "made a decision" to "let" God into my life. Growing up in a Presbyterian church, I encountered a different lingo. There was more an assumption of faith in Christ among those who attended the services.

My experience was more a gradual, progressive enlightening from the beginning as God showed Himself to me and drew me to Him. In retrospect, I am overwhelmed and humbled by the fact that it was always God who sought me first. Sinfully human and unworthy apart from Him, as I now know I am and long before I understood it, trusted in it, or loved Him back, God accepted and loved me. It was all God and none of me, to His praise and glory.

Most Sunday afternoons, from as early as I can remember, my parents would pile the four of us kids into the Ford sedan and make the weekly drive to my grandparents' home on two acres in the east edge of Claremore, Oklahoma. Grandpa Skidmore, even after moving to town, had made sure he had room to continue to grow fresh vegetables and fruits of all kinds.

Though every inclination in Dad that might have drawn him into farming had been squelched in his youth, he now understood better the consequences of poorly kept gardens and the resulting meager produce in the Depression years. He had made his peace with his dad's harshness. Now they enjoyed conversations about new varieties of fruit trees and hybrid improvements in tomato plants. We all looked forward to dinners at Grandma Skidmore's house, especially in the summers, when Grandpa's gardens were at their peak and a wide assortment of fresh vegetables found their way to the table.

Restless as much from hunger as from a desire to see our grandparents, we siblings kept asking "how much longer?" from midway through the half-hour trip until we finally began to recognize the outskirts of the little town northeast of Tulsa. The ride seemed especially long if we knew cousins were waiting for us.

Every week, a different mix of aunts, uncles, cousins, neighbors, and friends gathered in that sometimes noisy but always loving Skidmore house. One of my first memories, certainly the initial recognition of something profound and spiritual, came when I was about three.

On the occasion in question, one of the grownups, though I'm not sure whether it was an uncle or a distant cousin, was playing the "I Got Your Nose" game with me. Pretending to snatch my nose, ear, chin, etc., with a snap of his fingers, he would show me, as proof of the steal, what I recognized even at three years old to be the tip of his own thumb between his two knuckles. Each time, I would giggle, "No, you don't! It's still here!" I would touch my nose, ear, and chin in turn to confirm that each part was still attached as before.

I remember considering as the game wound down what it would really be like to lose a part of my body and being struck by the significance of what I had discovered. I actually remember looking at various parts of my body and thinking "This is my hand, but it's not really me. This is my arm, but if it were gone, I would still be here."

I don't remember who was at my grandparents' house that day, what the occasion was, or what happened before or after. For that matter, I don't remember very much else at all about being three years old. But I remember, as though a spiritual snapshot had been taken, that moment when I fully understood that "I" was somehow completely separate and different from the sum of my body parts. I understood that the real "me" was on the inside. I was much too young to have been taught that by anyone or to have understood it with my brain or intellect. It was a truth that came directly from God, a spiritual understanding.

Though we kids were in Sunday school and church most weekends with Mom, the vast majority of those lessons and sermons came and went without having any immediately perceptible effect although I like to think they were building a good foundation.

When I was 8-9 years old, however, another incident happened that not only was significant but also has served as a frame of reference during many subsequent periods of self-doubt and discouragement.

I don't remember details of the message delivered by Rev. James DeFriend in John Calvin Presbyterian Church that morning. I had been doodling on the back of my church bulletin in boredom, having been trained to at least be quiet if not interested and actively listening.

It must have been about mission work. Probably my first realization that there were people who actually spent their lives giving their talents and their full-time attention to God's work, helping people. Though not really concentrating, I was hearing snippets of what was being said.

I was moved, unexpectedly, out of the selfish world of Me to a completely new kind of perspective: thinking about what other people need instead of what is pleasing, entertaining, comfortable, or convenient for myself.

I don't remember any specific words that Rev. DeFriend uttered. What I do remember is that at one point during the sermon, in response to something he said, I felt a tingling sensation pulse through my body. Suddenly attentive, I felt compelled to stretch out my hand and trace around it. I heard the words inside my head, in a voice that didn't seem my own, *"This is my hand, and God's is in it. Together, we will go throughout the world making people happy."*

I heard the exact message a second time and felt obliged to write it down, right there on the back of the bulletin, around the margin, next to the hand I had traced. I didn't understand exactly what the message meant, but I knew it was important. And I was sure it was from God. As if I'd been let in on some secret about my own future.

The bulletin itself, for years kept in a small box of early private writings and other treasures, is long gone. But that moment, in that church service so many decades ago, when I heard God's voice speak to me, was so real, so profound, and so supernatural, that I've never forgotten it.

Time and again since then, I've been tempted to question my circumstances, second-guess my decisions, or doubt God's plan for me. But those words He spoke to me, in language which matched my age at the time, He repeated to make sure I'd remember them. And I do. I can close my eyes even now and hear that gentle reassuring message in my head. Those simple words to the child I was are a reminder that He is and always has been with me. And that He doesn't make promises He doesn't keep.

# Destiny Derailed

Weeks and months turned to discarded calendars, filled with the tedious and monotonous stuff of daily life. My school years were like those of millions of other people: inconsequential and unimpressive for the most part, with a few well-placed 'aha' moments and events that ultimately changed the course of an otherwise yawn-worthy existence.

One of those moments came in Kindergarten when it was discovered I could sing. Every week, I would memorize the latest little ditty learned in music time. I relished performing each new tune, with hand motions in synch, for my parents. Soon, I was garnering larger audiences as my mother coaxed me to perform for relatives who gathered for birthdays and holidays.

Reluctant at first, I was soon wowing this very biased group of grands and greats who would show their appreciation by tossing coins my way. These were mostly dimes and quarters, but occasionally a 50-cent piece appeared, and on a really good day, if Grandpa was in the audience, a silver dollar.

My sisters still teasingly tell a Cinderella rewrite of me being the charming child, entertaining and winning over the adoring adults and their change purses, while they (neither ugly nor step-) were slaving in the kitchen after holiday meals, doing dishes. It was a rather over-stated case, if you ask me. It didn't really happen *that* often, but over the course of several years I did hone my skills, graduating from the obscure "Sammy Put the Paper on the Wall" to better known pop tunes on the radio like "How Much for that Doggie in the Window?"

Third grade would not have been a terribly significant year, at least school-wise—there were no high stakes tests or reading expectations like today—were it not for my transition from Bluebird to full-fledged Campfire Girl, an after-school activity. I was a city kid who was mostly interested in reading books or watching movies about pioneers, cowboys, and Indians. Long before I knew the significance of the misnomer of that latter term and the realities of Native American existence, I relished the exotic idea of living and cooking by campfire—as long as my mother could go along and we didn't have to spend the night!

Almost laughed out of Campfire Girls because of my reticence toward camping, I was not inclined to continue in the group the following year. But my friend Mary talked me into it, saying there would be lots of other fun things to do since her mom was going to be the leader.

In fact, fourth-grade Campfire Girls was indeed a memorable time, with swimming lessons at the YWCA and skating instruction and parties at Parkey's Roller Rink. I made a few good friends and gained some confidence. I was a fair skater, crossing my right foot in front to maneuver the curves in the oval floor, and I might be able to swim to safety, if form didn't count, although diving was a bust. A belly buster, that is. The gravity in my lower body was so great I could never learn to fling my head down first and thrust my legs up in the air above it. Fortunately, most of the other girls weren't much better, so I never stood out too much.

The culminating event for 4th grade Campfire Girls, however, was to be a talent show. That was a huge departure from the other activities that we had done as a group. Taking my Sunday afternoon living room show to a real stage? With only me on it? Where people I had never seen before would be watching and listening?! That wasn't my idea of fun. In fact, it was terrifying!

Although part of me very much wanted to risk it, with fantasies of me in the place of my teen idols, I didn't have the courage or self-confidence to sing in front of anyone who wasn't my relative. No way! It wasn't going to happen!

However, my will-not-take-no-for-an-answer Campfire leader, Alice Way, absolutely insisted that I could, should, and *would* do it. There was no use arguing with her. So, I entered the talent show and practiced for weeks in advance. It was long before the days of Karaoke or 'track tapes' to sing along to, and there certainly would be no live band. Just me. Singing a cappella. What if I started it too high or too low and couldn't reach all the notes? What if I forgot the words?

The night of the show, I waited my turn backstage, going over the lyrics in my head. I tried to wipe the sweat from my palms on a part of my dress that wouldn't show. As one by one the other kids danced, played the piano, or read a poem, the knot in my stomach got increasingly bigger. Then, I heard my name, and I froze in panic. It was too late to back out. They were already politely clapping for me. I gulped, and with a gentle nudge of encouragement from Alice, I walked around the curtain.

I tried not to look at the auditorium, full of people staring at me expectantly. I breathed deeply and opened my mouth to chirp the first nervous notes. Then, an unexpected calmness came over me, and I belted out Brenda Lee's "Sad Movies Always Make Me Cry" just the way I had rehearsed it a hundred times.

It was so quiet after that last long note ended that I wondered for a split second if the audience liked it. Then, thunderous applause and shouts of "Encore!" broke the silence. It was exhilarating to know they loved my song. I was euphoric and immensely relieved it was over at the same time, but as I tried to leave the stage, Alice was pushing me back yelling for me to sing another song. What?! I hadn't rehearsed any other songs!

But there I was again, on stage, with the audience cheering me on. I should have stopped while I was ahead. I brought the house down at the Wonder Bread Bakery Talent Show with my rendition of Brenda Lee's hit song. Then, I followed the petite idol with the only song I could think of that I knew well enough: an ill-chosen perky but anti-climactic "Froggy Went A-Courtin'."

My sense of heightening an audience's experience may have been undeveloped, but the rush of adrenaline and the roar of the crowd were not lost on me. It became clear, at least to me, after packing the gymnasium for the school talent show at the end of 5th grade and landing a lead role in the 6th grade play a year later that I was on a course for sure stardom.

and waited for others who crowded up front to check the list. I wasn't sure I even wanted to look, preparing myself for mediocrity. But in spite of my unsureness, a pesky ray of hope for something more just wouldn't die a decent death.

When the throng of hopefuls had thinned to just a few, I forced myself to get up and walk to the wall by the door. The nauseous waves that accompanied every heartbeat were making me seasick as if I were walking a plank and about to jump into a wide sea of disappointment to my doom.

Scanning the results in reverse order, I started with the least desirable group. If I expected to see my name there and did, I wouldn't be disappointed. It would just confirm my expectation, right? Not there. Well, that was a relief! At least, I wasn't at the bottom of the food chain.

As my eyes moved up the page to the next group I was already consoling myself. It wouldn't be so bad. Middle of the road was better than dead last. Wilson, Wescott, Thornbrough, Thomas, Stiles, Stevens, Smith, Shallenberger, Scott. Wait, what!? I read through the list of S names again, feeling the impact as my stomach did a belly buster into the ocean of disbelief. Mine was not there. How could that be!? How could I not have made *any* of the groups?!

Just as tear ducts were filling my eyes to the brink of overflowing, that relentless little voice of possibilities told me to keep looking up. My knees almost buckled and my heart leapt out of my chest to see Skidmore wedged right there between Snodgrass and Shelton in the top list on the board. I had made *the* group! I would be in Chorale, the most elite, most sought-after, most prestigious choir in the large mid-city high school.

It all fit. I was closer than ever to reaching my life's purpose: to travel around the world, singing and making people happy—just as God had told me five years before. I had finally come into my own, and my destiny was back on track! That school year, and that chapter of my life, ended in a giddy swirl of anticipation that God had something exciting and wonderful for me just around the corner.

I'm glad I had those weeks of bliss before the death knell came in June. The small company, Bell Oil & Gas, where my father had worked for as long as I could remember, gave notice it was relocating. We were moving to a town an hour north of Tulsa, called Bartlesville, Oklahoma, where I would start my high school prison sentence in the fall.

# Podunk *Where*-ville?

To the good people of Bartlesville, I belatedly apologize for the condescending, crabby, cranky attitude I had toward their fair city for almost the entire duration of my term, uh, stay there. It wasn't their fault, (or *was it*?) that my dad's employment stability chose this precise moment in my life to lure our family to the brink of civilization.

Moving to a dinky, podunk town I had barely heard of to begin what was supposed to be the best years of my life, high school, was unthinkable! I did what any other unenlightened teenage self-professed starlet would do. I sulked, moped, cried, and stayed in my room for most of the first three months.

But who could blame me? Upon enrolling in my sophomore-year electives, Chorus and Spanish I, I'd found out that there were no auditions for the chorus. Great! Anyone who wanted to could just sign up for the class. I knew what that meant, and the first week at the brand-new Sooner High School confirmed my fears. Instead of traveling with the elite Will Rogers Chorale choir in Tulsa, I was stuck in a chorus class with people who couldn't carry a tune in a dump truck, forget the proverbial bucket! The "music" grated on my ears as much as the whole scenario in Bartlesville grated on my soul.

In hindsight, I realize the move to Bartlesville was a huge adjustment for everyone in the family. Mom had gotten her secretarial skills through the FDR work program and had begun her career—though I never heard her use that word—with the newly formed Social Security Administration in Washington, D.C., back in the '30s, but she and Dad had married in 1943 and then started a family after he was back from the war. Mom did what most mothers did in that era. She stayed home to raise the four of us. After Kenny, the youngest, was in junior high school, she went back into the workforce after almost 20 years. Now, just two years later, she was leaving a job with the Department of Human Services in Tulsa and hoping the transfer would come through to work in the Bartlesville office.

My oldest sister, Karen, had just gotten married in June, after one year at Northeastern State University in Tahlequah, Oklahoma. She was living at home again for a time while her new husband was serving out his active duty in the Navy. Her trauma consisted of being separated from Wayne and had little to do with the move to Bartlesville, except that she was lonelier than ever. Her circle of high school friends had naturally become less important.

My next older sister, Dubie, had finished her junior year at Nathan Hale High School in Tulsa just a few months earlier in May. Now she was a senior, and instead of enjoying her last year of high school with her friends, she would have to spend it with a group of total strangers. She was the only person for whom I felt sorrier than for myself, and even then, not fully.

Kenny had to make the adjustment, too. He was in his last year of junior high, so he was forfeiting upper classman status as well. At least, by the time he entered high school, he'd have made the transition and would have a group of friends here to enjoy it with, even if it was in a different city.

But at almost fifteen, I wasn't very good at looking outside myself to see that everyone in the family was struggling and making adjustments. I was convinced my situation was worse than anyone's. For a while I was inconsolable.

My siblings and I drove back to Tulsa on weekends as often as our parents would loan us the second car. The used Ford Falcon was a shared vehicle which Mom and Dad had bought specifically for teenagers driving to school and/or work. They were at least aware enough of their teenage children's painful adjustment to the move that they made the exception for the Falcon's use. Those trips back to Tulsa on the weekends served as an important buffer for a while. They helped alleviate the suddenness of the changes and soften the drastic feel of the move. After all, not just our friends but our very lives were back there: our history, our potential, and our dreams.

As the months of commuting went by, however, I began to see how impossible it was to keep that part of my life—those friendships—really vital and alive on a long-distance basis. The fabric of life is imprinted in the ample space of day-to-day activities, not the weekend margins. My relationships in Tulsa were losing that quality of daily interwoven strength. Each visit would reveal new things I was not privy to: comments, looks, and funny mishaps "you just had to be there" to appreciate. And I wasn't. I was becoming more a memory that interrupted their lives on weekends than an actual part of them.

Thankfully, God was merciful and brought me into contact with another girl in the chorus class who was also shy and reserved. Sharon Howard was a soprano, and I was an alto. We were well into the fall season, and the date had been set for the winter program. We'd been practicing the lineup of songs for a couple of weeks, but some of the numbers were difficult and a few kids weren't getting the challenging intervals. So, the director, Mort Cuplin, asked Sharon and me to help some of the other students who were having trouble learning their parts.

For several weeks on designated days, Sharon and I worked with individuals and small groups in the class, which helped solidify the overall sound of each section in the chorus. It also afforded me the opportunity to get to know her better.

Separated all those months by four sections of risers, I had seen Sharon but had never heard what a beautiful voice she had. She was quiet and kind, and when she smiled, her eyes, magnified through thick glasses to twice their actual size, lit up her whole face.

I think now she must have seen or sensed the inner pain I was struggling with. Perhaps she had experienced some of the same left-out feelings I was now having. In fact, maybe Mr. Cuplin had recognized, as any good teacher would, that we both needed a boost to our self-esteem. Perhaps he saw that we could help each other in non-musical ways while we were helping others in the chorus with difficult parts that somehow came easily to us.

In any case, Sharon seemed much farther down the path than I was of discovering inner worth and a sense of belonging to something bigger than just a group of high school socialites. Whatever she had been through, she was stronger for it. Strong enough, confident enough, and loving enough to recognize and empathize with someone else's pain. God bless Mr. Cuplin for having the insight to put us together.

At the time, however, I was entirely focused on my own outward circumstances. I saw the whole experience in this new over-sized small town as a great loss, a giant step away from my destiny. A detour. It would take me many years to realize the enormity of what I had gained from the transplant to Bartlesville. I didn't recognize, while I was living it out, the extensive inward overhaul I needed. And I certainly didn't understand yet that God is perfectly willing to seem like "the bad guy" for a time so that He can do the good work, the transformative work, in us which will ultimately bring us closer to Him and secure our joy long-term.

At least for now, after meeting Sharon, a ray of hope was beginning to break through. All our hours of hard work—singing those parts over and over with our classmates—had finally paid off. I remember thinking after the last note was sung of "Lo, How a Rose" at the Winter Concert, *Wow! I didn't think we could ever sound that good!* A part of my soul was starting to heal.

Maybe this place called Bartlesville wasn't so God-forsaken after all.

# Godsend

It was refreshing and good for me to be around someone that knew who she was, what she liked, and what she stood for. It was definitely not cool in my former circle of friends to still be in any kind of scout organization. I had been in Blue Birds and Campfire Girls in elementary school and had friends who did their stints in Brownies and Girl Scouts in younger years. But from mutual unspoken fear of rejection, we all assumed we had outgrown that phase by junior high school.

Now, in high school no less, this new friend Sharon unapologetically invited me to a camping/hiking event with her scout troop. Not having much to lose socially, I accepted, with only a few misgivings from my non-camping Campfire Girl experience. Why not give it another try?

Though not a fan of group campouts, especially the overnight variety, in the third grade, I had loved the summer weeks spent on my uncle's farm outside Yale, Oklahoma. I'd ridden a horse a few times and climbed a tree or two, which was more than some city-slickers. I had hiked up and down the sandy banks of the Cimarron River more than once and had really loved those connections with nature and the rural setting as much as the time spent with my cousins.

Both my parents had rural roots. Mom had grown up a few miles outside of Coalgate, Oklahoma, in Cottonwood, a small community where only a dozen or so families lived. Dad was born and raised in Oolagah, Oklahoma, a small town not far from Claremore, where his folks later moved and where I remember visiting.

In spite of my parents' connection to farm life and rural settings, however, I was a city kid, born and bred. The summer visits to Uncle Raymond's farm and the weeks spent in Cottonwood with my grandparents were the closest I ever came to spending any substantial time in the country, away from my home in the near-half-million metropolis of Tulsa.

Living full time with the small-town feel of Bartlesville was new to me. It reminded me of being at Grandma Harney's, where everyone knew everyone else—except me. Sometimes, Grandpa would take us into town to get a soft-serve ice cream at the Dairy Queen. Everyone we saw knew Grandma and Grandpa and stopped us to chat and fawn over Freda and Matt's grandbabies. I was fine as long as one of my grandparents was nearby. Let them disappear around a corner, and I panicked! That's almost how I felt, thinking about the hike—like I was going into Sharon's familiar home territory not knowing anyone—and I hoped I wouldn't be as clingy as I'd been as a child.

I was actually looking forward to the hike and to connecting with something I felt in my family, in my blood, even if not in my experience. I had romanticized the pioneer days as a kid and loved the Little House on the Prairie books by Laura Ingalls Wilder. Living in the country, like on the untamed frontier, seemed a harder, but simpler and more rewarding way of life. Maybe this hiking-and-camping event would be good for me.

My connection with the quiet woods and countryside near Bartlesville that fall did much more than remind me of my family's connection to the land and more than just fill a weekend on my social calendar. That weekend camping trip turned my attention away from myself and allowed me to find a simpler kind of contentment. In an autumn forest. In a sunset mirrored on a placid lake. In the song of meadow larks flitting about in a field. Those things held a quiet beauty apart from and oblivious to my anguish. The initial allure of nature in the hidden splendor of the campground was something I could share with my new friend Sharon.

Over the course of my high school years, when I was struggling to come to grips with many issues, Sharon was a godsend. A real, true friend. We spent time together at her house and mine, getting to know each other's families. With time, we both felt comfortably a part of the other's. We had sleepovers and went to a few football games though we were neither huge fans. We studied together when we had a common class. We took walks, and I shared with her the secret location of my sanctuary rock. I'd discovered it while wandering the fields near my house.

Sometimes, we baked cookies. To this day, I still do something I learned from Sharon while baking together. I use a clean finger to rake out the last drop of the egg white from the shell, so as not to waste it— evidence of the Depression-era-parents we also had in common.

A few times, we even went to church with each other. One Sunday, I visited with Sharon's family at the Methodist church, which became the subject of a later conversation. Sharon and I talked a lot. She was someone I trusted with my most vulnerable thoughts and feelings. She was a good listener and never judgmental, just interested and concerned.

Something in the sermon that day had brought up a question I'd wondered about for years. I thought this Jesus must have really been a great man, so willing to put our needs ahead of His own, but I still didn't get why it was necessary for Him to die on the cross in order to help us get to heaven. If He was the Son of God and God loved Him, why would He make Him do that? Why didn't God protect Him, and save Him with us?

Sharon's answer, though to this day she doesn't remember having such a clear understanding herself at the time, was my first realization, at least on some level, that Jesus' death on the cross was not just to *help* me but to substitute himself *for* me, dying in *my* place.

I didn't have an inkling at the time that God's only begotten Son was the only One who could meet the standard of perfection and bring us into the pure and holy presence of God. Nor that the only way to do it was to sacrifice Himself and die a sinner's death—which He didn't deserve—so that we who put our trust in Him could live the resurrection life in Him forever with the Father. I didn't understand any of that yet.

Suddenly, at Sharon's explanation, it all became so personal. It felt so harsh and unfair—for Jesus and for me. It was shocking to think that I was so bad I deserved to *die*! Sure, I'd been critical of people and maybe unfair at first in my assessment of some kids at school. Okay, I'd been pretty snooty about not wanting to be in a choir you didn't even have to try out for. And I had felt kind of guilty a few times when a group of girls

# Faith or Fear Showdown

I realize looking back that my mother was a woman of great faith. She didn't talk a lot about God or expound on her beliefs in Christian terms and phrases, and she didn't usually waste time trying to persuade people to her way of thinking. Rather, she had an underlying belief, an inner assurance, that everything was going to work out okay. Even when upsetting and very troublesome circumstances would arise, she would always say, "This, too, shall pass."

When I was younger, I didn't find much comfort in that phrase, but when I finally got old enough to ask her about what it meant, she helped me understand—I did find it comforting—that at some point, this present trial, this problem that's eating away at me, will end. There will be a resolution, a time when I'll look back on it, when it'll be in the past, and when I will have gotten through it somehow. That underlying attitude of "Keep the faith, it'll all work out, you'll see" had a tremendous grounding effect.

Mom loved going to church. She'd been the one who initiated our attendance when we were kids at the newly formed John Calvin Presbyterian Church. The church was meeting in the neighborhood school near our house while their building was under construction. She had walked the half-block with us every Sunday to the McKinley Elementary building for Sunday school and church services. When the congregation finally moved into the finished church several miles from where we lived, we attended there as long as we lived in Tulsa.

True to her custom in past years, Mom quickly found a Presbyterian congregation nearby, and we started attending services on Sunday mornings shortly after settling into our new house in Bartlesville. Mom was not one of those people who felt compelled to be in church every time the doors were open. She did, though, volunteer occasionally, and we participated in a few special activities. Except for weekends when we were out of town, we always started our week with 11:00 church on Sunday.

It had been okay with me most of the time, except as a teenager. More than a few Sunday mornings I would much rather have slept in. Going to church in those years was something I knew I *should* do more than something I really *wanted* to do. Though there were messages that were meaningful or gave me pause momentarily, going to church mostly meant going through the motions. By Sunday afternoon, I was comfortably back to the world around me.

Mom had laid the right foundation taking us to church from the time we were very young. It had been a positive experience and had helped lay the foundation for who I was as a person, at least as much as I could know myself at 15. Yet, there had always been something inside me that was at odds with my faith in God.

On one hand, I genuinely believed in God and had been taught early on that He loved me. I had gone to church regularly ever since I could remember and had received an uncanny message I supposed to be from God. I'd spent time thinking about that message and wondering how my life would be affected by it. Feeling drawn closer to God, I'd been baptized, the sprinkling kind, at the John Calvin site in Tulsa, at the age of 12. I was as grateful as any 12-year-old can be that someone named Jesus had died on a cross 2,000 years ago, though for reasons I was not clear on at the time, so we could go to heaven. I was a regular kid with a good, solid, loving family and home. Generally speaking, I'd always been happy.

At the same time, unexpected fits of fear would possess me without a moment's notice. I wasn't just afraid of going to hell, heaven was equally as frightening, simply in the unending, eternal, everlasting aspect of it. I just couldn't understand the concept of something going on and on and never ending. When I would think of eternity, even in heaven, and imagine eons of time passing, it terrified me to think there would still be eons more. On the other hand, the idea of time stopping with nothing beyond was just as horrifying.

From society's perspective today, I would probably have been diagnosed with panic attacks and prescribed medication to deal with the anxiety disorder, a treatment I don't doubt has helped many people profoundly. In one way, however, I'm thankful now we were not so "advanced" in those days. It seems that with every step forward academically in medicine, it gets that much easier to take a giant step backward spiritually. Nowadays, we tend to look for any remedy to quickly ease the discomfort of what we are experiencing without paying much attention to, or worse, outright ignoring, the root of the problem.

The attacks were real alright. I just didn't understand them or how to control them all those years ago. Forty-five years would pass before I would become familiar with the verses in Hebrews 2 which perfectly described my experience. All I knew was that the episodes of fear that had come over me periodically since I was four years old were getting more severe and lasting longer.

Visiting the Methodist church with Sharon and the conversation we'd had afterward caused me to spend more time trying to come to grips with what I really believed. During that time, I had another bad attack. I had many over the years, but this one stands out in my memory for a couple of reasons. It was the worst one yet, and it was a turning point.

When I would feel one of the spells coming on, I would hide in my bedroom or lock myself in the bathroom so no one in the house would witness it. I don't remember specifically what triggered this episode. I only remember being frantic to get into the bathroom and lock the door as I began to feel the nauseating sensation in my stomach, desperate to conceal the panic rising inside me as my heart raced.

With the door firmly shut and locked, I could roll with the wave of sheer terror that I physically felt surging up through my legs, torso, and engulfing my head. I broke out into a cold sweat, beads running down my face and arms. The moisture on my chest wet my bra and shirt. I sank trembling onto the closed toilet lid, dizzy and rocking in agony.

As the physiological manifestations racked my body, my mind raged equally on the inside. *You know you are going to die, everyone does!* I imagined myself inside a dark, stifling coffin. *It will be dark, with no air.*

I saw the wooden box in a hole with dirt being shoveled on top. *You'll be buried there for thousands of years. Your flesh will rot, then you will turn to dust. No one will know you were ever there or that you ever existed.* I tried to fight back and make the thoughts stop. *God help me! I can't do it by myself!* You *have to help me get through it!*

With death at the center, the 'it' was becoming an all-encompassing whole of everything I feared, everything I doubted, everything I needed to understand but didn't. I was devastated at the realization that I could do nothing myself to change any of it. I couldn't stop myself from dying, yet I couldn't face the experience, the process of dying, on my own.

I felt a sickening swirling motion inside me that was taking my breath away as if I were on a whirling carnival ride, but instead of the euphoric, giddy feeling of a rollercoaster, it felt like something was sucking the very life out of me as in a tornado or a giant whirlpool. I was afraid I would pass out and had a flashing view of my crumpled teenage body found lifeless on the bathroom floor when someone finally had to break the door down.

Though my ears seemed deaf to any real sound, the words to the psalm I'd memorized in grade school came to mind *"...though I walk through the valley of the shadow of death, I will fear no evil: for Thou art with me..."* I wanted those words to be true for me, but I knew I couldn't stop the fear any more than I could stop death. Even if God was there to help me through the valley of death, *I would be in heaven forever and ever....*

As the wave of nausea began to swell again, I searched frantically for some thought of comfort and felt completely, utterly helpless. I couldn't die. I couldn't live, not this way. I couldn't do anything. I didn't know anything. I was limp, almost lifeless at the bottom of a deep cosmic drain that I knew any moment would fill with black, rushing waters that would wash me under. It was the lowest point, emotionally and spiritually, of my entire life, either before or since.

Another scripture came to mind, *"...for God so loved the world..."* I wasn't even sure of that anymore. But I had to believe it. If I didn't have that to hold onto, I had nothing. No hope. No help. No escape. In the lull between waves, I had gotten up off the closed lid, afraid I might actually fall off when the next one hit. I was leaning over the sink now with my head and right shoulder resting on the mirror behind it for support. I remember that moment when I challenged God, *"You said you loved me. I don't know if you really do or not, but I have to trust you. You're the only one who can help me. If you love me, take the fear away. I don't want to think about it anymore. When the time comes for me to die, you'll have to help me through it. I can't worry about it anymore."*

There it was. The truth. I couldn't do anything about any of it. I *had* to trust God to do it for me. I had no choice. I washed and dried my face and sank down on the edge of the tub just to compose myself. Exhausted and empty, but finally calm, I got up and left the bathroom.

It would be several decades later, teaching at a private school and preparing for a lesson on the Hispanic celebration of Día de Muertos (Day of the Dead) that I would finally understand my deliverance from the fear in a new light. In my study and research for the lesson, I'd come face-to-face with Hebrews 2:14-15, a perfect description of me at 16. I wondered how much of my trauma could have been avoided if I had been equipped with a knowledge of that verse:

*Inasmuch then as the children have partaken of flesh and blood, He Himself likewise shared in the same, that through death He might destroy him who had the power of death, that is, the devil, and release those who through fear of death were all their lifetime subject to bondage.* (New King James Version)

GODSWAY

# Relentless Pursuit

For as long as I can remember, I have always believed in God, and prayed to Him. At first, my prayers were the God-bless-Mommy-and-Daddy type that were modeled at bedtime when I was very young. The list got longer of people I wanted God to bless as my awareness grew of an expanding circle of friends and family members.

After a while, even I tired of the long lists of names passing as a prayer. I was glad when Mom explained that prayer is talking to God and suggested we talk to Him about some other things, too. My prayers changed in vocabulary and substance with my age and interests.

After the message from God at nine years old, I continued to believe and pray, with more thought behind it. *"This is my hand, and God's is in it. Together, we will go throughout the world making people happy."* I wondered a lot, especially in the months after I received the message, about exactly what it meant and how we were going to make people happy. I loved the idea that God and I would be holding hands, and sometimes I let my imagination take me to all the exciting places in the world we might travel to.

By the time I was nine, I'd already been entertaining at family gatherings for years. I loved everything about it—the singing, the performance, the applause, and of course, the financial reward gained from doting relatives—the whole package.

I'd also discovered at the Wonder Bread Bakery that year, when I'd given the performance of my life to an auditorium full of the families of my Campfire Girl peers, that I loved the exhilaration and roar of the crowd cheering for me. Since the other-worldly message had come so close to my public singing debut, I always assumed that "making people happy" meant singing. It was the only thing I knew so far I was really good at doing.

Even by the age of 14, I was still working under the assumption that singing would always be a key part of my life. I wasn't anywhere near mature enough spiritually to understand God's timing and the years of waiting on Him that are often involved.

My prayers and faith matured to match each age, without any enlightenment along the way as to the logistics of how the message would play out in my future. I just had to take it at face value and continue to live my life. And continue to wonder occasionally how it would all work out.

I recognized as a teenager that most things were still out of my control, so when there was something especially important that I wanted or thought I needed, I prayed for God—selfishly most of the time—to work it out for me.

I had prayed fervently, for example, for a particular boy to ask me to the 9th grade prom at Hamilton Jr. High School my last year in Tulsa. I'd been pleasantly surprised that God answered that specific prayer in spite of the fact that the boy had been seeing another girl in the months just before. That had at least confirmed that God did answer prayers and reinforced the idea that He loved me.

Then, He answered my prayer about making the elite choir at Will Rogers High School, where I would have attended had we stayed in Tulsa. I was excited about going to Will Rogers because the extra performances, the local exposure, and the publicity surrounding Chorale would surely help advance my career. It was before the days of social media where an individual can build a platform by making connections with other people. Outside of a picture and article in the local newspaper, though probably just of the whole group, I couldn't envision exactly what the publicity would do, but I just knew it would have to help someone notice me.

It seemed like the path was finally coming clear and I was moving out of the 3-year junior high phase of being a complete unknown. God seemed to be confirming I was on the charted course to *"...go throughout the world making people happy"*—through singing, naturally. Being accepted into Chorale indicated I was headed in the right direction again, finally! Toward the bright lights and my real purpose.

Then, God had slammed on the brakes, changing the whole course with the move to Bartlesville. He had heartlessly ripped me out of the familiar world that was just beginning to open up to me. He had randomly dropped me here, in this little town called Bartlesville. What was I doing here? How was I supposed to understand that the God I thought loved me had torn me away from everything I loved?

It was such a dramatic way to shut me down, this shift just 50 miles north of where my life had been, like a slight miscalculation that threw everything out of kilter in a cascading effect, and threatened to wreck every secure part of a half-built skyscraper, all the potential greatness about to be dashed to bits. It seemed unnecessary, even cruel. It didn't fit with anything I thought I knew about God. The move didn't feel very fatherly, either, whether caused by my earthly father or allowed without intervention by my heavenly guardian.

The first few months after the move were gut-wrenching. Just seeing a group of girls laughing together in the hall was a slap in the face that taunted, "But you don't have any friends! Your friends might as well be a thousand miles away! You'll never fit in here."

My new circumstances and everything about the move seemed so contrary to what I had believed about my life up until that point. I'd thought I was close to God, but none of these changes made sense. My friendships, my dreams for singing, my work with Him—everything—seemed irreparably shattered. I felt I must be missing something. I needed God to help me understand where I had gone so wrong.

Once I'd gotten past the initial and very real mourning stage, I began searching for my Creator around me in His creation. If I'd been so wrong about God before, then I wanted to know who He really was. On the hike with Sharon's Girl Scout troop, I'd found a serenity in the quiet countryside, which was at least a beginning.

After that, I sought out time alone with nature whenever and wherever I could. I needed to find a way to understand what was happening. A way to put some of the pieces back together into something recognizable. I was trying to make sense of this new phase of my life, grasping for evidence of the loving God I was struggling to hold onto. I had to get back to basics, back to something I understood. I needed the salve of quiet to bring peace to my brain and my broken heart. I had to find a way to believe it was all still going to be okay.

In a new subdivision on the east side of town, our house bordered a vacant field. On walks exploring the terrain, I had found a large, mostly flat rock comfortable enough for sitting on. It afforded a pleasant view from atop a slightly raised portion of the undeveloped section of land. This boulder in the middle of a field, even with streets and traffic lights a quarter mile away, had been the next-best thing to the country when I was stuck in the middle of town. It became a secret refuge, a sacred place.

Many afternoons, I would go there just to think and to listen. The sounds of birds chirping and the wind rustling through the tall prairie grass had brought calmness if not real peace to my spirit. At least, I could breathe again. It made me almost feel that all was right with the world—at least the rest of the world. I wasn't sure how my own smaller world fit in, but I had this new sense of peace that it was all somehow in God's hand. I thought of Mom's go-to phrase often and finally understood its truth. This too *shall* pass. It really will. But it didn't stop me from wanting to know *how* or from trying to speed up the process.

On rainy or cold days I would stay in my room, not to sulk anymore but to stare out the window into the same field or into the sky, searching, thinking, and praying for God to show Himself to me. I had so many questions about what this move really meant and how things would be different from what I used to think.

But how do you force God to speak? My desperation to know was not impacting God's timetable of responding to me. There were no answers coming, and life was going on all around me. Whether I liked it or not, I was thrust into the middle of it, just by being. So, I'd done my best to keep living, to keep putting one foot in front of the other even if I didn't know the path I was on or where it would lead me.

I also kept talking to God, asking Him to speak to me, to reveal something, or to give me answers. For a year-and-a-half, even when

He wasn't saying anything back, I asked and prayed. Finally, I began to understand it was part of the process. My earnest search for answers, for truth, and for Him was an important part of the equation. Even though I couldn't control how or when—or if—He would respond.

A waiting season is hard when you're young and don't have the foundation of a trusting relationship to shore it up. The bouts of fear and anxiety had come to a head in that culminating attack. I'd been forced to trust God by virtue of my total inability to change any of it. I'd had no choice. I hadn't trusted Him because I already knew He was trustworthy, but rather because I was simply out of all other options. If I wanted to survive, and I'd felt that literally, I had to give it up: the fear, the need to control the panic, the desperation to stop the thoughts, the longing to understand, and the need to have answers to questions—all of it. I couldn't carry the storm around inside me anymore.

The pressures of school and the uncertainty about my general situation were not lessening or changing. In fact, a failing grade in Chemistry and putting on weight added stress, but once I'd actually challenged God's love for me in the bathroom that day and declared that I had to trust Him—even if it was my last resort—to get me through all this, I began to see little ways He was helping me.

In the daytime, my rock in the field was my sanctuary, away from my siblings, the household, and the busyness of everyday life in a 6-member family. At night, finding a quiet place to escape to was not as easy. The discovery of critters lurking close by in the field had come many months before when Mom found a quite large rodent swimming in the toilet bowl at a bathroom break in the middle of the night. What a commotion that was! So, no, the rock was out of the question after dark.

I found an alternative solution closer to home. Sometimes in the evening, when I felt overwhelmed studying or frayed for other reasons, I'd go outside and sit on the brick half-wall that surrounded our front yard. It was beyond the range of sight or sound inside the house yet not far enough away to risk unwanted encounters with the nearby nocturnal world in the field. I'd think or muse about a question. Sometimes, I'd pray. Other times, I'd mull over a poem or song lyrics. Once in a while, I would just enjoy the night and be quiet. Waiting for God.

Even with the newest anxieties, when a thought would start to trigger another fear episode, I went to a wall inside myself: a safe place where I was being held in and could run no farther. I would remember that I didn't have to worry about that anymore. God was taking care of it. The fear would subside and no longer spiral out of control into a full-blown attack.

I was always thinking, searching, and meditating about God and what I believed. It's hard to draw conclusions, however, just through reasoning, as I found out. At least, I was truly searching now with an open mind, not just going through the motions or trying to get God to do things my way. I really wanted to find the one true God—to know the truth even if it was different from what I'd always believed.

One night on the wall stands out in particular because it was the first time I got an immediate, direct answer to a question. We had been reading Dante in literature class. I wasn't familiar with the idea of purgatory, and it made me curious again about what heaven was really like. My daddy's valiant effort years ago still wasn't cutting it as a substantial answer. Were there degrees of heaven? Different parts or places in heaven?

I was sitting against a brick post between sections of the wall that night, looking up at the vast number of pinpoint stars and a hazy half-moon in the black velvet sky. It was so incredibly beautiful and so mysterious at the same time. I remember pressing God again for answers, *"Is heaven beyond the galaxy? If I could travel far enough into outer space would I eventually find you, God, out there somewhere in heaven? Where are you?"*

Just moments after that emphatic question registered in my mind, I felt something like a tender tap on my chest from the inside and heard the gentle answer, *"I'm right here."* A new understanding washed over me. Suddenly, I felt profoundly silly to have been searching for God out in the vast distance of space. What an intimate, deeply personal, and reassuring response from God! I now finally understood that I didn't have to search Him out in some mysterious, remote celestial abode. He was right here, inside me all the time.

After that night, I felt a connection with God like I'd never felt before. Even though I still didn't know why we'd moved to Bartlesville or what the direction of my future would be, I finally *knew* God loved me. I was armed now with the understanding that He was right here with me day in and day out, through every situation, in every moment. The things I didn't know or understand, the issues that used to be so fearful and cause such anxiety, simply didn't concern me much anymore. I knew He was constantly on guard for me. It was somehow all under control.

GODSWAY

# Relevance

As a young child, at least from Kindergarten on, my parents and other adults had coaxed and prodded me into singing for them. They praised me and applauded me, encouraging me to continue to perform, which I loved doing, all through grade school.

Once I arrived at Hamilton Junior High in 7th grade, it was a different story. The vocal music teacher, Emily Schultz, was a no-nonsense instructor, who was a consummate professional, dedicated to music and to excellence. She gave piano and voice lessons outside of school in the evenings and on weekends, and several of the kids in the glee club and chorus classes were her private students. She was their mentor and encourager, like my parents and Alice Way had been for me.

Mrs. Schultz already knew that pipeline of talent personally. She expected them to do the solo parts and be the leaders in the choir. Outside the group she was already familiar with, she was never very open to others trying out for solo parts. Or maybe it just seemed that way to me because I was no longer the one being noticed and coaxed.

Either way, like most women and girls in that era, I had never learned to be assertive. For almost three years I lacked the nerve to speak up. I never broke out of that passive rut of waiting to be discovered. I stayed on the margins, overlooked, all through junior high school, like an understudy waiting in the wings for her chance to shine. It was probably more my own timidity than any real attitude on the part of Mrs. Schultz that held me back.

But after forcing myself to try out for Chorale and making it, I was finally starting to prove my worth not just to Mrs. Schultz and the kids in the glee club, but to everyone at Hamilton and mainly to myself. I did have some real value. I really could hold my own with a group of other singers. I was looking forward to high school. I couldn't wait to show the people in Chorale and the entire Will Rogers vocal music department all that I was capable of. But of course, that never happened.

From the first moment I stepped into Sooner High School in Bartlesville, I struggled to find my place, my relevance. I found myself in a world that was suddenly bigger than just my nurturing family, my childhood friends, and the schools I had left behind in Tulsa. After standing silently in the shadows for three years at Hamilton, I longed for acceptance and recognition now from these strangers, but they all seemed to know each other and didn't particularly need a new friend. I was wise enough to see that from their angle *I was the stranger.*

I was still an outsider. I hated how it made me feel. I hated wanting and needing their approval. I shouldn't need it. If I were sure enough of what I had to offer, confident enough of who I was and my purpose for being here, in Bartlesville—and more broadly speaking, on the planet, alive— that would be enough to help me fit in and be happy. I truly didn't want to be miserable. I just wanted to be accepted, a valued part of something, but it seemed I was farther away from that reality than ever before.

It was like playing Wahoo and having a marble which had made it almost all the way around the board. Then, just when it was so close to being safely at home, being knocked off by another player who had landed on my spot and sent me back to the beginning. I didn't know who had taken my place in the Chorale choir, but I didn't feel like I had it in me to start over again from scratch.

I withdrew into my room, as much as I could at least, sharing it with two sisters. I searched for solace in a bag of chips or a momentarily comforting bowl of ice cream at night before I finally succumbed to tormented sleep. I was miserable, a fish out of water, floundering, stuffing my body with taste-good foods and at the same time feeling the life ebbing out from the inside.

I was also searching for the God I knew in the midst of all this change. I was in need of a new reference point and was willing to rethink what His message that I'd received so many years before could mean. I found my rock in the field nearby and regularly sought Him there, entreating Him to speak to me and help me find my way again. Though for months and even years I didn't have any real answers, those quiet hours of meditation opened up a mind frame of receptiveness and a well of creativity in me that I had never known was there.

I was an empty cup, filling up with so many scary painful feelings, aches, longings, and loneliness that I had never felt before. I wanted to pour them all out in desperation. After many months, I began to write down thoughts, poems, and observations. Once my dad had taught me a few chords on his guitar, I wrote songs, too. Rudimentary as those first writings were, a hunger began to grow inside me for expression and for real music again. Whatever new direction I was headed in, this time I would have *my own* songs to sing.

My sophomore year was somewhat typical of any beginning high school student of the time, with English, Algebra I, Biology, Spanish I, and Chorus on the slate. My overall high school experience, though, revealed several things about me, academically, in addition to the inner turmoil and search for self that was playing out.

First, it turns out, I was really good at Spanish. I'd been intrigued for several years when Karen would use phrases around the house from her high school Spanish classes. I'd been adamant about taking Spanish as soon as I could to figure out what she'd been taunting her "baby sister" with for the last three years. She'd delivered on numerous occasions one particular phrase with squinted eyes, a menacing grin, and such dripping sarcasm, that I knew she must be saying something like 'Be quiet and mind your own business, Twirp!' I found out soon enough that the accurate translation was "Pass the butter, please."

I'd counted on taking Spanish at Rogers, and at least the move hadn't canceled that part of my plan. Sooner High offered Spanish I, II, and III, and I was completely on board for the 3-year duration.

I loved the language and the culture, thanks to one of my all-time-favorite teachers, Suzanne Sparks. She had traveled to several Spanish-speaking countries and had taken many groups of students with her, always coming back with new treasures to show and stories to tell.

I can still smell the faint odor of stale cigarette smoke that surrounded her. I can see her wide grin and her reddish-orange lipstick and hear her husky laugh. I can see her hands moving erratically in exaggerated gestures, bracelets jingling as she would relay some funny incident from a recent trip. The personal anecdotes and authentic realia—postcards, souvenirs, ticket stubs, photos—from her own experiences brought it all to life. I loved everything about Spanish.

I also had a real knack for it. Pronunciation, grammar, vocabulary, and the varieties of Hispanic culture—the whole nine yards—just came easily to me. I felt drawn in that direction. As much as I loved singing, I'd never had any formal musical lessons, either vocal or instrumental. I knew I didn't have the music theory background necessary for a music major, but I had found something else I was equally as good at: Spanish. I was sure halfway through high school that Spanish would be my major in college.

Second, there was a direct correlation between my academic success and the ability of the teacher to keep me interested and help me understand the concepts accurately. (Duh!) Mr. Baker was my Biology teacher sophomore year, and I loved his class. He was young, funny, and passionate about living things. He made it interesting, and I did well.

In May, when I was enrolling for junior year classes, I saw that Mr. Baker was teaching Chemistry the following year. It was a no-brainer. Science was not really my forte; it was too precise and analytical for the new-found creativity that was budding inside me. However, I had to have another credit in that department to graduate, and I might as well get it over with my junior year so I could lighten my senior year load. It was either Physics with a teacher I didn't know or Chemistry with a funny, good teacher I'd already had. Done! I was all set for Fall, rounding out my schedule with American Literature, Geometry, and of course, Spanish II and Chorus.

Fairly early in the fall, however, it became clear that Mr. Baker was not nearly so passionate—and possibly not quite so knowledgeable, either—about chemistry. The experiments and formulas were getting more difficult all the time, and he wasn't as good at explaining things clearly as he'd been in Biology. I didn't understand the homework well enough to figure things out on my own, and I wasn't doing well on the tests. By mid-term, I was on the brink of failing Chemistry, which only made my other insecurities more acute.

I had always made good grades in school, and now that was changing along with everything else. I would much rather write a song or poem than memorize formulas or lab experiment procedures. So, it wasn't easy to keep my nose to the grindstone. Honestly, even on nights when I really tried to concentrate and study, that chemistry book was better than any sleeping pill on the market to knock me out cold. I was starting to feel entirely *un*done!

With my falling grade in Chemistry class, I was feeling anxious and struggling not to panic over school. I would soothe myself with a snack when I wasn't concentrating well or take "a break" and eat something to mull over a difficult concept. When I got sleepy studying, I'd go to the fridge for something cold to help me wake up. The overindulgence with food was starting to show. I was putting on weight, failing chemistry, and still trying to keep it together emotionally and spiritually.

It was the following spring that I had visited Sharon's church and was still pondering the theological ramifications of our subsequent discussions. Perhaps it was that heightened level of overall anxiety about a wide range of issues—my weight, my grades, my beliefs, and my quest to figure out my future—my relevance—which brought on the culminating panic attack.

In the weeks that followed my challenge to God, I didn't notice any sudden change. Life went on at school as I finished out my junior year. I managed to pull a D out of Chemistry after almost failing, so at least I didn't have to retake a science credit. I did well in math, thanks to a solid background in Tulsa and a great teacher here at Sooner High. I finished strong in my other classes as well, so my grade point average didn't suffer greatly.

My senior year came. I was enrolled in Spanish III, World Literature, Chorus, and Music Theory. I was done with what educators now refer to as STEM classes: Science, Technology, Engineering, and Mathematics. I knew I didn't need any additional classes in those areas for my Spanish major, so I focused my time and energy on subjects I enjoyed more. My classes were fewer but still rigorous, and I relished them thoroughly.

The creative juices were flowing more strongly than ever. In my spare time, I was writing, playing guitar often, and transferring some of my inspiration to creative writing projects in Spanish and English classes. For one assignment, I recited an original poetic composition in Spanish to a short instrumental track from The Good, The Bad, and The Ugly, called "The Sundown," by Ennio Morricone. It was my first attempt at the trifecta—combining the three areas of interest I was developing—Spanish language, creative writing, and music. It felt like a true accomplishment and was received with high praise from Mrs. Sparks and others.

Sharon and I still hung out together in the evenings and on weekends even though we didn't have any of the same classes this year. Life had settled into a much more comfortable routine than I had thought possible in this little town two years earlier.

Concerned about my chubbiness with senior pictures coming up, I'd started on a new weight loss program Mom had heard about for her and me to do together. I don't remember the name of the product or much about the regimen except that I had to chew a caramel and drink a cup of hot liquid thirty minutes or so before every meal. It was easy enough to stick to. The caramels, while not like the Kraft kind that you melted for apples, weren't bad, and I quickly discovered I loved coffee, long before the Starbucks days!

The weight was dropping off, slowly. Prom and graduation came and went in a flurry of anticipation, then relief. My life was coming back into balance as I made plans to room with Sharon in the fall at Oklahoma State University in Stillwater.

My life certainly had not gone in the direction I'd thought it would three years earlier. However, with a sense of new inner strength and the assurance from the night on the wall that God was still with me, I had an expanded understanding of my value and what my contributions might be in other areas besides music.

I was looking forward to leaving Bartlesville and, for the first time in a long time, to my future in general. Something in me recognized that God, even though He wasn't answering specific theological questions yet, was at work in my circumstances and yes, in me, too. I was not the sulking 14-year-old who had arrived here three years ago. I was someone very different, finally free from that inner prison.

GODSWAY

Then, junior high school swallowed me up. Though I tried out and made the glee club, I was a small fish in a larger lake of talent. Thanks to my Dad's road-trip music training, the harmony parts implicit in the alto section came easily to me, but given my sudden awkwardness in my new surroundings, my voice blended in a little too well for my taste. No one noticed me. No one was impressed. No one was asking me to sing for them.

My confidence was shaken, and I certainly wasn't going to assert myself. What if I made a mistake? What if I tried for a solo part and didn't get it? So, I sat back undiscovered for three years, envying those who tried and got the coveted parts and hating that I was too reserved and unsure to even attempt it myself. It was an important lesson in *not* being the center of attention, a waiting season.

Toward the end of 9th grade, however, about to go off into the scary world of high school in a shroud of complete anonymity, I had a dilemma to face. The vocal music director from Will Rogers High School was coming to my junior high to hold auditions for placement in the various choirs and singing groups in their music department for fall classes. I could play it safe and just enroll for the general chorus without auditioning, or I could finally muster the courage to lay it all on the line and try for one of the elite groups.

After some agonizing deliberation, I came to the conclusion that it was now or never. I had to find out if I was really any good or if it had always been, after all, just a circle of supportive friends and relatives who thought so.

The day came, and it was finally my turn. With nervous knots in my stomach and a dry pastiness in my throat that I feared might render me soundless, or worse, force me to swallow involuntarily in the middle of a prolonged note, I sent up a plea that my nerves wouldn't show and that I would be able to do my very best. Then, with the memory of that magical sad-movies performance buoying me, I calmly opened my mouth and sang from the heart as I had not done in three long years.

A week or so later the results came in and were posted on the choir room bulletin board. I stood back, as I had so often done in recent years,

I'd gotten to know made fun of Mrs. Schueler's Olive Oyl hairdo in World Lit. I had laughed and gone along with the fun even though I felt bad for the woman. It *was*, after all, one ugly, out-of-date coiffure! But come on, everybody was that way, right? I wasn't *that* bad! *Die* for being insensitive and rude?! I wasn't so sure about any of this.

I was fortunate to have Sharon to talk to. I needed to bounce things off a good listener in order to process the new questions which were forming now more rapidly than I could find answers for—about my beliefs, my faith, and my path. About who God was, why I was here, and where I was going. All of this new-found confusion fed into my old issues with fear. And it was about to get a whole lot worse.

# The San Bernardino Touch

With a renewed though still uninformed faith in God, I entered my freshman year of college in that late-teen stage between the self-absorption of adolescence and responsibility of adulthood. A new sense of anticipation accompanied my continuing search for answers as if I were on the verge of finally discovering my own personal path, my true destiny, after feeling derailed and confused for so long.

I understood there were far more important things in life than the short-sighted preoccupation with styles and who-is-dating-whom of the college coed stereotype. I wasn't concerned with any of that. I had been intrigued by and drawn to spiritual things, things of God, more than ever since that night on the wall in Bartlesville. My writing after that event had also taken on elements of my faith and my search for truth.

Early in that first semester in Stillwater, one of the sophomore girls in Willard Hall heard me playing the guitar and singing. Sharon was in class, and I supposed I was alone in that part of the hall, so I hadn't bothered to close the door completely.

I heard a tap, but before I could respond, a head with silky dark brown hair thrust itself through the crack and a tall lanky girl in blue jeans and a sweater vest introduced herself as Shelley. Something in the song she had overheard piqued her interest, and her curiosity got the better of her.

In that first stimulating conversation, I learned that Shelley played guitar also and sometimes sang at the church she attended. It was the first time I had ever talked with anyone other than Sharon about so many things I held dear: music, God, and personal faith. Shelley told me about the unconventional campus-based ministry called Believers Fellowship and invited us to check it out. We did the following Sunday.

It was a small non-denominational church that met in a rented Case Study room on the second floor of the Student Union. It was like nothing I had ever experienced in the Presbyterian Church in which I'd grown up. There was no offering plate passed, no choir to join, no altar call, no Sunday-best dress code. In fact, there were no guilt trips at all!

There was just this group of believers who were genuinely fond of each other, truly full of joy, loud with heart-felt singing, though not always on key, and insatiably absorbed in the study of the Bible. We loved the authenticity of the whole experience and returned the next Sunday and the next.

Sharon, Shelley, and I soon formed a trio, dubbing ourselves with the snappy name The Willard Girls—as if identifying our residence hall lent some sort of credence to our performance—and for the next four years took our turn in the rotation, performing special original music in the Sunday service every few weeks.

We attended several Bible studies regularly, and we had met some kids who were also involved with Campus Crusade for Christ, so we went to some of their gatherings as well. God was opening up his Word to me, revealing his Truth, and so many things were clicking into place. He was answering, straight from the Bible, so many questions I'd tried to figure out all through high school.

I was like a paper towel at a coffee spill. I couldn't soak up the richness fast enough. It was a time of tremendous spiritual growth as well as musical creativity. I was learning basic Biblical truths and coming to understand things, not through meditating upon the issues but by actually learning what God already said about them!

While I was growing in knowledge, I was also learning how to trust Him for specific needs, stretching my own faith, and no matter how small, or trivial it might seem to someone else, God showed me on a Spring Break trip to San Bernardino (and countless times since) that He knows our heart's desire and does care about and provide for even the small things—sometimes in supernatural ways. I shouldn't have been surprised after the night on the wall, but again, I was blown away.

It seemed an endless trek from Stillwater to California even in what was at the time a top-of-the-line Greyhound bus, complete with tiny toilet in the back. Sleeping was iffy, so I read most of the way. I devoured many of the Epistles in their entirety, for the first time understanding that these were actual letters written to real groups of believers about what they had gained in Christ and how to build up their faith.

That first image I had from Colossians 2, of the count of accusations against me taken "out of the way"—nailed to the cross—attached itself to my soul. It has stuck with me ever since.

During that week-long Campus Crusade for Christ retreat, we were following a rigorous schedule of Bible studies, training sessions, and worship services. Meals were sandwiched in between, and there was practically no "down" time until late in the afternoon.

Even though I had made the trip with several friends from Stillwater, the camp directors assigned roommates, pairing people who didn't already know each other so that we would all get acquainted with new people and not just stay in our familiar little cliques. Luckily, since the move to Bartlesville, it wasn't nearly as difficult for me to make new friends as it had once been.

After the first day or two, new friendships were forming, and kids were starting to explore the surroundings during their free time. Some had discovered a place nearby that afforded a breathtaking view from above the campsite.

My friends and I wanted to see it, but it would have been quite far and profoundly unpleasant to make the hike up the mountain in the afternoon sun during the hour of free time before the evening meal. So, we decided to get up a couple of hours early and go before breakfast the next morning. We planned to meet at 5:30, take the hike, and be back in camp before the 7:30 last call for breakfast in the dining hall.

Since my high school days in the field sanctuary near my house, I felt at home being surrounded by nature and eagerly anticipated the hike the following morning. As I was getting ready for bed that night, however, I realized Shelley had the alarm clock. I'd thought we would be rooming together, so I hadn't packed one. There was a clock in my room, but no alarm. Normally, there was no need for one.

Campers were startled into action each morning by the loud clanging of a sunrise bell. Like backwards pajama-clad mice we scurried into the spotlight at the sudden loud clangor. Tomorrow, however, I would need to be awake at 5:00 a.m., long before the noisy din started, while my roommate, who had declined the dawn rendezvous, would be sound asleep.

I was not a morning person even under normal circumstances. I knew I wouldn't wake up on my own in time to meet the group in spite of how much I wanted to see the view. I wasn't sure what to do, but I remembered a comment made by one of the group leaders earlier in the day about not being afraid to ask God for what you need and trusting Him to provide. I didn't know if this would count, but as I went to bed, I simply asked God to help me wake up in time to meet the group if He wanted me to see the view. Then, I went to sleep trusting He would work it out.

The next thing I remember is waking up to a gentle but very distinct touch on my right shoulder. With sleepy, half-opened eyes I looked around expecting to see my roommate who I supposed had decided to go with us after all. I was about to mumble my thanks but realized there was no one standing there. I searched the dimness and saw she was still asleep in bed across the room. Then, my eyes went to the clock. It was 5:00 exactly!

I dressed quickly, thanking God, incredulous that He had answered my prayer so literally. As I drank in the splendor of the dew-drenched sunrise over the peaks from a perch overlooking the lush green valley below, I was awe-struck at God's magnificent creation and heady with the realization that the same God who had created the San Bernardino Mountains had come personally to awaken me so I could share them with Him.

# The Mexican Train

The following summer, in 1970, I had the unforgettable experience of going with several of my friends from Stillwater to a 6-week Bible institute at Chula Vista in Cuernavaca, Mexico. It was sponsored by the Hispanic arm of the Campus Crusade for Christ ministry. Bible study, in a Mexican resort for six weeks?! Count me in!

I began building my case with Dad, successfully making the point that I'd be learning things I would use the rest of my life. And what an opportunity to practice Spanish! As it turned out, he didn't really take much convincing—how do you say no to a college-age daughter who wants to study the Bible and be able to practice in her chosen field at the same time?

Though we had an occasional weekend outing, the first five weeks were packed with intense Bible study. We had great discussions in class and sometimes continued them with fellow attendees during the short breaks. I cherished those snippets of time getting to know other people from Mexico and all around the Spanish-speaking world, who also loved and pursued God.

I was a dry sponge, expanding as I soaked up the daily sensory and spiritual input, like an elixir my soul had always craved. It was a pleasant cultural eye-opener to learn in our little resort dining hall that people drank whole glasses of watermelon or cantaloupe juice for breakfast. Somehow, I wasn't as surprised by the papaya or mango extracts. I came to love the fresh tropical nectars, pan dulce, and fried plantains of those quiet early morning breakfasts.

The last week, after all the classes and training sessions were over, was set aside for real sight-seeing. It was a spectacular bonus, to top off what had already been an incredible summer. We strolled through quaint narrow streets in the hilly mining town of Taxco, where instead of silver, I got a floppy suede hat to remember it by.

We saw the tourist beaches and the inner city poverty of Acapulco in a rented jeep. We swam in ocean water a postcard blue-green shade, where I discovered in a much too personal way the effects of getting caught in an undertow.

Last, we took in the museums and open markets of the historical capital, Mexico City. I bought souvenirs for family members and friends back home, and splurged on a *requinto* guitar for myself. I'd bargained such a great price in the San Juan market that I couldn't pass it up.

Though I was an avid gum chewer, I did have to turn down the boys in the street outside the market hustling every tourist who walked by, "Señorita, quieres chicle? Especial for you, solo ..." My Spanish was not great yet, but I knew the price he was asking for a small cube of gum was no bargain. I'd spent all I could afford to spend and maybe more.

When it came time, in fact, to make arrangements for the flight home, Shelley and I discovered that neither of us had enough money left to pay for the plane tickets that had been reserved for us. Exploring alternate transportation possibilities, we found the only thing we could afford, even pooling our money, was two 3rd-class train tickets to Nuevo Laredo and two bus fares from the border to San Antonio, where a friend lived.

From there I don't remember what the plan was—I think to call our parents and say "Help!" So much for responsible adulthood! For me, though, getting to experience some of the regional flavors of Mexico *and* acquiring my very own Mexican-made guitar in lieu of a comfortable first-class plane ride home seemed a worthwhile trade off. I had little inkling that the seemingly anti-climactic trip home would become instead the capstone of the summer.

The train ride north from Mexico City to the border was long, hot, and wearisome. While the rest of our Stillwater buddies flew stateside in comfort, Shelley and I were in a 3rd-class boxcar with very few seats at all. Most people were standing up. We were surrounded mainly by poor Mexican farmers, some with wives and children, and a few with animals. These rural workers, common country folk, would get on the train in one small village and ride to another *aldea* an hour or two away. The railed serpent slowly wound its way northward, stopping in every dusty town and village along the track in what felt like a time-warped, slow-motion western.

After a while, we settled in and got accustomed to the noises and smells of 3rd-class. At first, we tried to catch a familiar word or two in the half-audible conversations going on around us, but soon they all blended together as background noise.

After the first 2-3 times, we hardly flinched when the rooster clutched in the lap of an old peasant woman would break free, squawk, and flutter a yard or two before she managed to snatch it again, scolding it in rapid, lispy, unintelligible Spanish.

The bathroom in third class was the barest of accommodations, to say the least. When I was finally forced to seek relief, I was shocked to find behind the door that said "Baño" nothing more than a hole in the train floor. I could actually see the tracks racing by through the opening! It was a good thing I didn't have money to eat or drink much.

As the hours wore on, our feet became tired and our stomachs hungry. When someone occupying one of the seats got off the train, another traveler who had been standing for a while would sit down. The rotation came our way a few times, but when someone with a child, or an older person got on, we would give the seat up again.

Every few hours, we would take a walk through the other cars just to stretch our legs and bend our knees in some kind of normal human movement and to get our minds off the tedium of standing still on the endless crawl to the border. We would amble the length of the train, looking longingly as we passed the dining car, since we couldn't really afford to buy a meal. We'd peer enviously at the comfortable groups lounging in the compartments along the way, and then turn around and go back 'home' to third class.

Thus we spent the afternoon, the evening, and the endless dark night. When our weary legs and feet would no longer hold us up, we finally allowed ourselves to slouch onto the floor of the car, dirty as it was. I didn't really sleep but dozed a few times until my head drooped so low I banged it on the prized possession I was clutching. I hoped the music that would flow later from the miniature guitar would be worth the long hours of wrestling and shifting its awkward uncased shape.

Morning came at last, but we still had 8-9 hours left on this snail train through eternity. Our empty stomachs were starting to gnaw loudly on themselves before we finally went to the dining car to see if the little bit of change in our pockets would be enough to buy anything.

We plopped down wearily in an empty booth by the door, at least glad to sit down on a cushioned seat. Perusing the menu with an eye to the small pile of coins on the table, we calculated, if our math and our understanding of the Spanish were correct, that we had just enough for one blueberry muffin. We would split it and hope it staved off the hunger pains until we got to San Antonio.

When we were ordering, however, the waitress hadn't understood that we only wanted one. She brought each of us a muffin. In our still-immerging Spanish we tried to explain that we could only pay for one and reluctantly sent the other one back.

A few minutes later, while we were still savoring the last crumb and tangy blueberry of our half muffin, the waitress reappeared. Two steaming stacks of pancakes, dripping with butter and syrup were clanked down in front of us. Thinking we must have really confused her, we began to protest that we had not ordered this. But she waved us quiet and pointed to a booth across the aisle and down 3-4 from ours. She reassured us in broken English, "Don't worry. Those men pay. It's for you." We were surprised and touched, so we waved to the two young men in blue business suits to express our gratitude. They smiled and nodded in return.

For a fleeting moment I wondered if they had ulterior motives and whether we should accept, but we were famished. The syrupy aroma quickly engulfed all doubtful thoughts. We labored over every buttery sweet bite of those delicious pancakes, prolonging the enjoyment of every morsel as if it were our last meal. When we were full and could no longer justify lingering over the well-cleaned plates we got up to leave the dining car and turned to thank the kind men again, but they were gone.

We never saw the gentle strangers walk by our booth to the door which was right behind us. How could we have missed them? Who were those generous out-of-place travelers? How could they have known our predicament? Why didn't they make any effort to meet us or strike up a friendly conversation? And why didn't they speak when they left?

We looked for them in all the cars to thank them again in person, but we never found them although we were pretty sure the train had not even stopped again in the interim. In fact, as we thought about it, we were perplexed that in all of our strolls through the train, we hadn't seen them anywhere before or after seeing them in the dining car. Discussing the strange occurrence in retrospect, their blue business suits seemed out of place among the sweat-stained shirts of the farm workers and the average-looking attire of the other train riders.

If their journey had been so short that we hadn't seen them anywhere else on the train, why would they *need* to have a meal in the dining car? It was a mystery we couldn't solve. So many odd things we couldn't explain! Were they really businessmen who got on and off the train in consecutive stops along that rural route? Or were they other-worldly messengers sent by God as evidence of His personal interest in our plight? Either way, they provided for us in a time of need when we were far away from home, foolishly out of funds, and in the company of strangers.

I don't remember much at all about the rest of the trip home—who met us, how we got back to Oklahoma—none of it. It's as though my memory is stuck at the place where this fledgling believer realized those men in blue had appeared suddenly in the dining car just when we needed them and then vanished inexplicably off the train. Who were they, *really?* I know what I think.

# Domani Mattina

The years of our lives are made up of strings of ordinary days between the knots of trials and triumphs. God is there through them all, even in the seemingly meaningless days and weeks that tend to roll from one into the next without notice, in a repetitive loop.

Too often, though, we don't recognize His presence or even think of Him unless a situation arises that is so huge we realize we can't handle it on our own. We shouldn't wait until we are at the point of desperation before we turn to Him—I learned that the hard way, at the tender age of 16—as if God's attitude were "Take care of it yourself if you can; I'm awfully busy, so don't call me except as a last resort." That is so far from the truth!

God knows the exact number of hairs on our head. Every wrinkle, every itch, every thought, and every worry. He knows when our faith is strong and when we struggle to believe. He wants us to dare to trust Him in the trivial things, even in those circumstances which by all appearances we can deal with on our own. He wants to prove His faithfulness. After all, if we can't trust God for the minor issues, how can we rely on Him any more easily for the huge crises?

Faith is faith, whether we are dealing with a small issue in the eyes of the world or a huge crisis. God is not looking at how large or small the world thinks our problem is. He knows it's important to us. He is looking at how we react to it—with fear of the worst or with faith in His love and goodness. That is what God is looking for—even that first baby step of faith toward Him—to which He always responds in His time and way.

I had learned from my circumstances in Bartlesville, searching and waiting for God, that I couldn't control His timetable. I learned He doesn't think like I think or do things the way I would do them or the way *I would like Him to do them*. But what I learned better than anything else is that when God *does* answer, when He does finally show up, it's in a way that is so profound and extraordinary that there's no mistake that it's *He* and *not I* working things out.

When He did start showing up—on the wall in Bartlesville and in San Bernardino—it helped me learn to relax and not get so worked up over every little decision, always trying to be so perfect on my own. Although I still need constant reminding, I learned to go with the flow because He's got this. Whatever "this" is in the moment.

There's a fine line between due diligence and being a control freak. Between faith and negligence. So, throughout college—well, throughout life really—I was learning to do what I could, seeking God's guidance, and when I had done all I knew to do in a situation, to let it go, and not worry about it. He would have to be the one to take care of it in His way and time.

In spite of my struggles in high school with finding my own relevance and finding my place in the world regarding God's purpose for me, I was not one of the typical college students who debated for the first two years about what to major in. My friend and first roommate, Sharon, for example, had oscillated among several possible majors, including botany and mathematics. I'm honestly not sure what she ever settled on. But that was never me.

I was one of those rare and fortunate young college entrants who from day one knew exactly what I wanted to major in. I had many questions about a multitude of other issues, but that wasn't one of them. The extent to which I had struggled in high school Chemistry, I excelled in Spanish. I knew that's what I wanted to pursue.

Suzanne Sparks had done much more than teach me the mechanics of the language. She had also instilled in me a love for all things Hispanic. Beyond the food and language, I was mesmerized by the differences within the wide umbrella of Hispanic countries. I had a profound desire to immerse myself in the deep culture and to interact with its native peoples in their own language.

I saw my nebulous future only in terms of doing something exotic and exciting and somehow interwoven with my faith in God and my love for Spanish and Hispanic cultures. The trip to Chula Vista in Mexico had opened a window of my imagination to a whole array of possibilities. For four years, I took classes in Spanish language, Spanish literature, Latin American history and political science, humanities courses in religion, and other things I was interested in, making sure as well to fulfill all the other requirements of my chosen field.

However, in the spring of my fourth year at Oklahoma State University, when I was close to completing the required course work for my Bachelor of Arts degree in Spanish with a minor in Latin American Studies, my parents began to ask about my future plans. I knew that the pesky question, what was I going to "do" with my Spanish, meant how was I going to make a living at it? I was still thinking in possibilities, but they were asking about game plan. I didn't have an answer.

I had been so engrossed in the actual studies that I hadn't really put much thought into whether there was a demand in the workplace, or in what capacity, for the skills I'd spend four years acquiring. When they asked me about teaching, I was entirely put off. I'd never even entertained the idea though I had loved being a mentor and teaching things to younger cousins growing up. I didn't really want to *teach* Spanish. I just wanted to *speak* Spanish and be around others who also did. I wanted to *use* it for some sort of real communication.

Imagine my annoyance when I discovered, after investigating the need for translators, there was practically no such work to be had in Tulsa, Oklahoma. In the era before oil businesses had expanded to Spanish-speaking countries and before other major manufacturers had outsourced production to those places, there was not much demand for foreign language skills here in Oklahoma, except in the classroom as a teacher.

Reluctantly, therefore, I succumbed to the pressures of practicality and stayed an extra year, "cramming four years of college into five" as my uncle teased me, in order to get my teaching credentials.

I saw it only as a minor roadblock. I was learning to trust God with more of the everyday decisions and saw this as something He had had a hand in whether I'd been aware of it or not. I assumed He had a reason. So, I threw myself into the educational coursework of teaching a foreign language: methodology, psychology, and technology—if mimeograph and laminating machines can qualify as that.

With that fall semester behind me, the next spring brought my student-teacher experience at East Central High School in Tulsa, during which I lived with Karen and my ex-deployed, now employed, brother-in-law, Wayne. That treasured time of bonding with my adorable 3-year-old nephew and 1-year-old princess/niece as well as the on-the-job training in the classroom went by in a flash.

That spring, I ran into Suzanne Sparks at an ACTFL (American Council on the Teaching of Foreign Languages) training. After catching up on the interim years, and especially after she learned I had majored in Spanish, she invited me to accompany her the following summer as co-sponsor with a group of current students she was taking to Europe.

I already had a teaching job lined up for the fall in Dewey, Oklahoma, and though I didn't have the several hundred dollars yet that it would cost me, I knew I would be able to pay it back. So, I borrowed the money to take the trip, knowing it was the chance of a lifetime.

The invitation was a decision on Sue's part which I'm sure she came to regret in some ways. I was not very much help to her, and in fact, was most likely a great additional worry! She will never know, however, what an important growth experience it was for me. I spent four weeks in Europe in the summer of 1974 that are encapsulated in my memory as if they are from another life.

The first two weeks of our trip were spent in three of the major European capitals: London, Paris, and Rome; the last two weeks we spent in Spain. The scenic and cultural phenomena I experienced in those marvelous cities would fill a volume in themselves, so rich and life-changing they were for me.

From the moment we arrived at Heathrow Airport, there were more things to see and do than we could cram into the short days: the Tower of London, West Minster Abbey, Big Ben and Trafalgar Square, Piccadilly Circus, museums, parks, art galleries, and my first encounter with roast duck in orange sauce in a quaint little underground pub and restaurant.

In Paris, we took in Notre Dame Cathedral and the Louvre. I was personally more interested in historical and learning activities over the overtly tourist destinations, so in lieu of the Eiffel Tower, I opted for the Place de la Concorde, Napoleon's Tomb, and the Arc de Triomphe. We strolled and shopped along the Champs-Elysees and the Seine River. I saw the man in person whom I've seen since in dozens of postcards, fishing from the bridge over the Seine.

In Rome, we saw Michelangelo's Sistine Chapel and Vatican City, the Colosseum and Circus Maximus, and Piazza di Spagna with the Spanish Steps. We enjoyed a hotel room with a window directly overlooking Trevi Fountain, where we threw coins and made the obligatory wishes.

The travel 'bug' became more a travel 'drug,' producing a euphoric and exhilarated state that connected and cemented a mosaic of sights, impressions, emotions, and experiences, some of which I only learned the significance of much later. The first two weeks went by in a blur.

The last two weeks in Spain were equally exciting, but since this anecdote centers around not a city *in* Spain but an event *en route*, I'll leave off the travelogue of the last fortnight, except to say the trip ended with a final souvenir I hadn't planned on. While swimming off the coast of southern Spain in Málaga, I was stung by a Portuguese Man O' War, the scars from which I still carry on my upper right arm.

On the European mainland, our travel between cities and countries was via Eurail, with pre-paid passes good for the entire itinerary of the trip. When it came time to leave Rome and head for the main attraction in Spain, we checked out of the hotel and made our way to the train station with a little time to spare before boarding. Sue advised us of our train and departure time and designated where and when to meet in the depot, then allowed us to browse the shops while we waited.

For safety in those pre-cell-phone days, we stayed in groups, and Suzanne kept all the travel credentials and Eurail passes with her. Shortly before departure time, one of the girls in my group discovered she was out of film for her camera. We went with her to a shop in the depot to get the film, but they didn't have the size she needed.

We reasoned that we still had time and surely we could find a shop or pharmacy nearby that sold film. We wandered in and out of several places along the street with no success until finally a local pointed to an unlikely looking store where we did find exactly the right kind of film.

Mindful that the time was getting close, we darted in the direction of the depot and retraced our path as quickly as we could. When we got to the appointed track, with a few minutes to spare, we thought, there was no train there. We looked around for Sue and the larger group but didn't see them. When we asked about the train leaving on such-and-such track for Barcelona, we were told no, and sent to another train on a different track, scheduled to leave in about ten minutes.

Phew! We were relieved that we hadn't waited any longer at the wrong track! We assumed Suzanne and the others had already boarded and we would find them once we were on the train. So, we got on board and wondered how to go about locating the rest of the group. We were still wandering through the train, peering into compartments looking for our entourage when we felt the train pull out of the station.

I remember feeling a moment of panic but reassured myself everything would be okay when we were reunited with the others. I can't describe the sick feeling in the pit of my stomach when we searched the last remaining compartments on the train and found no Suzanne Sparks and no high school Spanish students from Oklahoma.

In those first few minutes, while my own insides were melting at the realization of our predicament, I was trying to remain calm and reassure the younger girls that everything would be okay. I was trying to make myself believe it. I thought about my simple prayer at San Bernadino. That was such a beautiful experience, but the consequences now could be infinitely worse than missing an opportunity to see a lovely landscape.

I started to panic, acutely aware for the first time of my responsibility for the teenage girls with me, and then something in me remembered I don't do that anymore. Instead, I prayed for God to show me what to do. I had messed this up so badly, and my anxiety was more for what the other girls were thinking and feeling than for myself. I knew I had to project confidence and faith. It would be fine. After all, we did have tickets; they just weren't with us.

We found a compartment with several empty seats and sat down to wait for the conductor. When he came around to collect the tickets, we would just explain to him what had transpired, and he would know what to do. Surely, this wasn't the first time such a thing had happened.

When the conductor finally came, he was not nearly as understanding and helpful as I had imagined he would be. In fact, he was quite put out. To make matters worse, he was yelling not in Spanish but in Italian. I could only make out part of what he was saying and guessed that since there was nothing else he could do he took Suzanne's name, begrudgingly, and would try to take care of it.

At every stop, when the conductor would come around to check credentials we would try to explain again, in English and broken Spanish, that we did have Eurail passes and why they were not on the train with us. The Italian conductors didn't understand us any better than we understood them, but it became clear that our story was not being passed on from one to the next. Each succeeding conductor seemed to be less sympathetic and more irate than the last.

The seething anger and frustration on their faces and the emphatic phrase "domani mattina!" rang through every shift. Both parties understood the gist of the situation, however: we didn't have tickets, and they were threatening to throw us off the train "tomorrow morning." No one wanted to actually throw us off the train, but no one wanted to be responsible for three stowaways either, when the next conductor came aboard.

It was clear to me from the beginning of this fiasco that only God was going to keep us from being put off the train and stranded in the middle of nowhere with no way to communicate with the local people or to contact Suzanne. So, at every stop on that 24-hour, almost 550-mile journey, I prayed the conductors would forget about us or have pity on us and let us stay on board to our destination.

I thought of that other long train ride, from Mexico City to the U.S. border, and how God had taken care of Shelley and me. I tried to take comfort although this seemed much more dire a situation. Over and over, after the explanations, yelling, and threats subsided, I thanked God every time the train started to move again, and we were still on it, until we finally reached Barcelona.

What a joyous reunion when we saw the familiar faces of our Bartlesville friends again. The addictive euphoria of travel had subsided, but something had taken root much deeper within me.

How could I have known that such a small thing as a rare type of camera film would cause such a huge near-crisis? I couldn't imagine what was going through Suzanne's mind throughout those long hours of separation. I could only put myself in a parent's place, if anything had happened to one of those girls, many years later when my own daughter was in danger.

Yet, by God's grace and protection three young American girls rode a train from Rome, Italy all the way around the Mediterranean seaboard to Barcelona, Spain without tickets and without being stranded or harmed. In spite of the odds, we were safe.

I felt relieved and empowered, making a mental note of things I would and would not do the next time I were in a similar situation. I also felt reassured and even freed by the knowledge of God's constant attendance in spite of my failures.

A large, terrifying, and beautifully intricate knot was tied on the string of my life during that summer in Europe. The threads of history and God's presence in the nations and through the ages came alive for me in a way that no museum could ever have displayed them and entwined themselves with my own faith and experience. I was overpowered by the magnitude of God's attention to the details and specific daily needs of the vast number of His individual children. That trip to Europe seemed like the end-all experience, but there was so much more to come that I had no idea of at the time.

# Let Go and Look Up

Riddle. What do hydroplaning to the edge of a steep drop off, threadbare tires on a dark deserted highway, vanishing Samaritans, and an out-of-control truck bouncing across four lanes of interstate highway have in common? Answer. I survived to tell about them.

Most people, if they drive long enough, eventually have a close-call story. However, when my travel tales of inexplicable narrow escapes and supernatural encounters mounted up so quickly in such a short span of years, my heart began to understand what my brain had known all along. Someone was watching out for me, and He was going to very obvious extremes to get my attention.

Within a period of four years, when I was a young single woman driving between cities in northeastern Oklahoma, Kansas, Arkansas, and Missouri, visiting family members and friends, on several occasions, extraordinary things happened and *didn't happen* on the highway, which kept me safe and helped me get where I was going.

The first of those episodes was during the year I taught at Dewey. I was in Tulsa for the weekend and planning to meet and ride with several friends from Believers' Fellowship Church who were driving back to Stillwater from Tulsa in spite of the rain.

The small campus-based ministry had not only served as a spiritual balance to the new-found freedoms of college life but had also forged deep, lasting friendships which were still important even though many of our close-knit group had graduated and left the university setting. BF was having a reunion picnic, and though the weather was not cooperating, we graduates who missed the connections with our other friends, were *not* going to miss it even if we did have to spend the afternoon inside.

We were driving west out of Tulsa along Highway 51 near the Keystone Dam when suddenly a simple lane change turned into an out-of-control slide down the highway. We realized we were hydroplaning at 65 miles per hour! More as a reaction than a well-developed spiritual discipline, we immediately began to pray out loud. In a matter of seconds, we skated across both lanes of traffic, fishtailed, and spun completely around, heading for the embankment.

However, instead of vaulting off the edge into the air as physics says we should have, the car came to an unexpected halt on the right shoulder of the west-bound lanes. We were facing east, opposite the flow of traffic, in a place where there was no fence or guardrail to stop us.

In amazement, we all got out to check the car and catch our breath. Peering warily over the edge into a deep ravine no more than a foot or two away from where the tires rested, we were stunned to see how close we had come to plummeting to the bottom. Possibly to our deaths. We all knew immediately there was no explanation for the excellent job of parallel parking other than divine intervention—angelic hands on the wheel. It may well have been a practice run for something that would come several years later and prove to be quite a bit more tricky even for an angel.

During those years, first at Dewey, then during stints in graduate school in Stillwater and Fayetteville, Arkansas I often drove to visit family and friends on the weekends, not thinking about the upkeep of an automobile. I wasn't trying to dare God or test His protective care. He had proven Himself faithful on numerous occasions already. I simply went where I needed and wanted to go, trusting Him and not thinking much about the used vehicles I drove, except to put gas in them.

Bell Oil and Gas, the small oil company which had employed my father and moved our family to Bartlesville just as I was entering high school years before, had merged with Vickers Petroleum while Kenny and I were still in college. My parents had been transplanted once again, this time to Wichita, Kansas. Thus, going home now simply meant going wherever our parents were.

One time, while I was well into my first year of a graduate assistantship at the University of Arkansas, I decided to go to Wichita late on a Friday night for a weekend visit at my parents' house. The shortest way to get to Wichita from Fayetteville, was to go northwest through a string of small towns in Arkansas, Oklahoma, and Kansas. It was a narrow two-lane highway, with very little traffic, which wound through the wooded hills of the adjacent northern corners of Arkansas and Oklahoma, and meandered northwestward toward the more open plains.

I noticed something a little different about the feel of the car that night but thought it was futile to stop and try to find the problem. I didn't know enough about automobiles to recognize it if I saw it. Besides, it was so dark I couldn't have seen anything, anyway. I didn't even have a flashlight with me, much less any other tools! My genius solution was just to keep driving. I would tell my dad about it when I got home.

The next morning Dad called me out to the driveway and showed me I had a flat. The other tires were so worn he could see the cords in the rubber behind what little tread was left on them. He looked at me incredulously and began, "I don't see how you made it..." He stopped, suddenly choked up. His eyes filled with tears, and still speechless, he put his hands together as if in prayer and pointed them to heaven. I'm sure he was thanking God for protecting me on the long, night-time drive from Fayetteville. I didn't really think so much of his reaction until years later, when I, too, had children driving. I know God used that instance to build my father's faith even more than my own at the time.

After that incident, Dad made a concerted effort to teach me about taking care of a car: how to check the oil and radiator fluid, how to change a tire, all the basics. I watched and listened intently, hoping I would remember it all if I ever had to do it by myself.

Sure enough, a while after that, I left Fayetteville, my old Chevy, and graduate school behind, unfinished for reasons of the heart too complicated to describe here. I had stayed a few days with my cousin Amelia in Tulsa but needed the sturdy foundation and emotional support of my parents. I decided to spend a week or two in Wichita to do some soul searching about the next step.

I was in a vehicle I hadn't driven much on the highway headed west, past Stillwater, toward the I35 North turn off, lost in thought. Somewhere in that lonely stretch of road, I was jolted back to the present. Kerblump! Blump! Blump! Kerblump! I pulled over onto the shoulder and got out. Just as I had suspected, where there should have been a tire, the wheel was separated from the pavement only by a rubber pancake.

Feeling some anxiety, I thought, "Okay, don't panic, here is where I get to see how well I learned about changing a flat." But after opening the trunk of the Audi, I realized that yes, everything *was foreign*. It was a strange-looking spare tire that didn't seem big enough to fit on the car, and the jack, if that's what it was, appeared to be nothing like the one I had practiced with in Dad's driveway. I couldn't figure out how to get the tire inflated or the jack to hook to the bumper.

After fiddling with it for a while I realized I was getting nowhere. It was still in the days before cell phones, and I didn't know how far I might have to walk to find a public phone or someone to help. I did know if I was very late, my folks would be worried, more worried than they were already.

Surveying the deserted expanse of concrete sprawling in both directions in the afternoon heat, I prayed that God would send someone to help me. I thought of the nighttime trek from Fayetteville on treadless tires and imagined how differently that might have turned out if I'd had a flat that night. I thought I was better prepared this time, but I still couldn't take care of it on my own. At least, this time it wasn't dark. I was thankful for that.

Only a few minutes later, an older man who looked to be in his mid-50s pulled over behind me and got out of his car. He asked if I needed help. I'm sure he saw the relief on my face as I accepted his offer and explained that I hadn't seen that kind of tire or jack before. I don't remember much about the conversation, just small talk about the difference in a foreign car. He worked adeptly, changing the tire for me as quickly and easily as if he'd done it a thousand times, and finally put the tools and flat back in the trunk. He made his way back to his own car, cheerfully dismissing my profuse expressions of gratitude with a hand in the air.

I walked around the front and got into the Audi. As I started the engine and signaled to pull out, I looked in my rear view mirror to wave one last thanks to the kind stranger, but there was no one there. I turned around in the seat to see where he could be. He hadn't pulled past and gone in front of me. He wasn't backing up to turn around. He wasn't *anywhere in sight*, even in the distance. I thought it was strange how quickly he disappeared and couldn't really explain it. In my eagerness to resume my own journey, though, I didn't give it much more thought, except to wonder if I'd expressed my appreciation well enough.

Later as I looked back on that incident and thought about how he had vanished so suddenly, I remembered the two mysterious men in blue on the Mexican train. As I compared the two similar disappearing incidents, I concluded that perhaps the kindly gentleman, who seemed like he'd been changing Audi tires longer than they'd been in existence, actually had just vanished, like the men in blue, having completed that particular task of taking care of me.

The most amazing road story, however, came a couple of years later. My Jesus-take-the-wheel experience happened a little differently than in the song. Lost loves and missed opportunities were things of the past, and I was absorbed in a new relationship and a new adventure. I was going back from Tulsa to Aurora, Missouri, where I was the owner and proprietor of the first 7-Eleven convenience store in the area.

Nowlin, my new fiancé, worked for MAKO, Inc., the company that handled the 7-Eleven franchises for a 4-state area: Missouri, Arkansas, Kansas, and Oklahoma. His job as a field rep kept him, well, out in the field, selling franchises, helping to set and stock new stores, and helping the new owners learn the ropes of the franchise business.

Being his favorite new franchisee, I got questions answered and problems solved a little more quickly than most other store owners. He came through Aurora as often as he could to check on things and help out, but it was difficult for me, even at 27 years old, to be alone in a small town so far away from everyone I loved. So, I came back to Tulsa to be with family as often as I could get employees to cover the weekend shifts. At the end of one such visit, going back to Aurora on a Sunday afternoon, something so extraordinary happened that I was never the same afterward, either physically or spiritually.

To avert the boredom and the blues, I had purchased a soft drink and some sunflower seeds when I filled up the gas tank before leaving Tulsa. I was somewhere between Joplin and Springfield, Missouri on a four-lane divided highway, contentedly spitting my sunflower shells into the by-then-empty cup and humming to my favorite 8-tracks of Boston and Little River Band.

I glanced down to the dashboard for a split second to check the speedometer, as I often did, since in my college years I'd been known to have a heavy foot once in a while. I'd done it thousands of times; everyone does—check the speed, look in the mirrors—it's a matter of good driving habits.

Yet, on that day, as I glanced down, at the exact same instant my left front tire hit something in the road that made the whole front end of the Ranchero jump sharply to the right. What could I have hit? There hadn't been anything visible in the road, and my eyes had only looked away for that one fraction of a second. As my brain was wondering what could have happened, my hands reacted in a jerking motion, trying to get the truck back in a forward direction. But the force of the sideways movement was too strong, and my reaction only sent the vehicle further out of control.

As I yanked in the opposite direction, the centrifugal force on the back end of the truck brought it careening in a circular motion as if spinning around an unseen center point. I was literally tugging on the steering wheel by now, fighting with every ounce of my strength to regain control of an automobile that was bouncing and swerving in all directions at highway speed.

The realization dawned on me that I was not going to be able to regain control. As if in immediate response to that understanding, I heard a male-sounding voice speak emphatically into my thoughts, *"Let go!"* I didn't know who was speaking or what the message meant, but still battling the steering wheel, I heard the command again, firm and deliberate, *"Let go!"*

Suddenly, though I could see no one, I knew the voice was telling me to let go of the steering wheel. (This was my "jumping off the building" moment.) I obeyed, releasing my grip and taking my hands off the mechanism entirely. For the next few minutes—I really don't know for how long—I watched a slow-motion theater through the windshield as the truck did a ballet dance.

The cars in front of me looked normal for a split second, until the scene changed to green grassy pastures with dots of cows that did their bit and quickly bowed away as the truck did another quarter turn counterclockwise.

My eyes fell on the approaching swarm of traffic, dozens of cars and trucks of all shapes and sizes, growing, coming straight toward me. It was indeed one of those instances when real time had been suspended and everything was happening in exaggerated retardation.

It was eerie, yet peaceful, to be a spectator watching the events unfold in that divinely choreographed scenario. I remember thinking, *"Ok, Lord, I guess this is how I am going to die. If this is it, I'm ready."* None of the fear and anxiety over death which I had experienced most of my childhood and adolescence was present, a testimony to just how far God had brought me in the last ten years. Here I was in the moment I had wondered about and dreaded for so long, yet I continued to look on serenely, prepared for impact at any moment.

Another full circle was complete, and then a pas de chat in the air, with the back end of the Ranchero pounding hard on the raised, grass median, bouncing my head against the ceiling. The dance continued, though now with other partners as we spun around and through the two lanes of traffic on the other side of the divided highway. Then, I remember feeling the difference of sliding through grass, compared to the pavement, and suddenly I realized the movement had stopped.

Not able to fully comprehend what had just happened, I shook off the dream-like state and looked around. As I was getting out of the vehicle, it took me a moment to get my bearings and understand where I was: on the wrong side of the highway, facing the opposite direction from where I had been going. After swirling and bouncing through four lanes of traffic, I had come to rest once again safely parked in the grass just off the right shoulder of the southbound lanes, in a small and very precise area where there were no highway signs, no fences, and no guardrails with which to collide.

Incredulously, I took note of the details and the enormity of the odds. Even though I already felt close to God, I was overwhelmed at the extent and power of His love and protection and the dramatic way in which He was willing to demonstrate it.

An 18-wheeler pulled in behind me. The driver scrambled down and rushed over to ask if I was alright. He offered to take me to a hospital or call someone. When I told him I thought I'd be okay and didn't need an ambulance or a doctor, he didn't look convinced, indicating that he'd seen me take some pretty nasty bumps. The anterior atlas vertebra in my neck that had been compressed in the head bump against the ceiling didn't assert itself until a year or so later.

At the moment, I was still in awe of the whole occurrence and didn't really feel any pain. In fact, I felt more than fine, I felt exhilarated and almost weightless as if my feet were hovering just above the ground. When he was sure there was nothing I would let him do, the driver started toward his rig, kindly warning me, "Okay, but you be careful now. That was a close one." With the echo of that protective, celestial mandate still reverberating in my head, I remember thinking, *You have no idea!*

That latest encounter was the one that helped all the other unexplainable events in my past come sharply into focus. God proved himself to me so undeniably and so supernaturally that day that in all other difficult circumstances since He has used the memory of that gentle, firm command as a reminder to stop fighting for control. To let go and look up.

# Brian's Bane

The variety of ways in which God shows Himself and interacts with us is remarkable. Sometimes, He is there in the small details, attending to relatively minor needs, just to prove that He is *not* "watching from a distance" but actively involved even in the minutia of our lives, responding to our faith in Him.

Other times, in trials and hardships thrown against us by the world and by the evil one, God is there guiding us through those painful, difficult periods, using things that were meant for evil and working them instead for good. He teaches us valuable spiritual lessons through them all along the way and helps us to rise above worldly troubles in victory. Individually, and as a couple, Nowlin and I have had our share of trials, like most of God's people.

During our engagement Nowlin had traveled a lot as a Field Rep with MAKO, and I had been busy with the Aurora store. Although these were important steps in the learning and skill-building process, we were homesick and tired of being away from each other and from family.

We were elated when we got the word that a new store was being built in Tulsa and the company would be looking for a new franchisee. Nowlin jumped at the chance to be in a store of his own, especially in Tulsa where we could settle down and enjoy being back home, and close to relatives. For most of a year, a whirlwind of activities surrounded selling my franchise in Aurora, opening the new store in Tulsa, getting married, and moving.

For several months of that transition year, I was still in Aurora, finalizing the sale and tying up loose ends while Nowlin was overseeing the setup and establishment of the new store in Tulsa. During those first months in Tulsa, he'd gotten acquainted with one of the regular customers whose office building was next door to the store.

Mike Greene was a half-blood Creek Indian (before the vernacular had self-corrected to Native American), the youngest of nine children, a bachelor, and the live-in caregiver to his elderly mother. A former school teacher, he was currently working for the Oklahoma Tax Commission as an unemployment claims judge.

When he wasn't traveling to hold hearings outside of Tulsa, Mike would come into the store most days at lunchtime to grab a sandwich and a soda to take back to his office. He and Nowlin had struck up conversations and discovered some similarities in their backgrounds.

On several occasions when Mike's bowling team needed a sub, Nowlin filled in for whichever team member was out of town; over the months he had found a new circle of buddies. The chitchat with Mike turned into a genuine lifelong friendship which, as the years would prove, made an impact on our family forever.

The Aurora store was finally sold, and Nowlin and I were married. We settled into our new circumstances, glad to be together and thankful for the opportunity to start building for our future.

It didn't take long, however, to discover that there was such a thing as working together too closely. We soon found ourselves at odds over small things due to our different personalities and styles of management. So, after the first year of running the store jointly, we decided it would be best if one of us stayed in the store while the other found employment elsewhere.

Since I had an Oklahoma Teaching Certificate and one year of teaching experience from the year in Dewey after the excursion to Europe, the obvious choice was for me to return to teaching and for Nowlin to become the sole proprietor of the 7-Eleven franchise.

I put in teaching applications at several school districts in the area, but so close to the start of the school year most places had already filled the vacant positions. I applied for and got a job teaching two sections of Spanish, Beginning and Advanced, at Tulsa Junior College several evenings per week. I planned to do some substituting until one of the school districts had a full-time opening, hopefully by mid-year.

A few days into the school year, however, I got a call from Tulsa Public Schools for a 4/5 position teaching Spanish, traveling between two different schools. It wasn't quite full-time, but with my work at TJC in the evening, I had plenty to do and enjoyed the long lunch break during the travel time between schools.

That was a happy but busy year. By the next fall, I had a full-time position with Tulsa Public Schools and didn't need to moonlight any longer in the evenings. Nowlin and I joined a bowling league and bowled together one night a week in a mixed league with other couples and another night separately on men's and women's teams.

I'd only been bowling a time or two in my life and didn't know much about any aspect of the game. I had zero skill at the beginning. I had to learn from square one how to hold the ball, where to stand, how many steps to take in my approach, and how to take my turn at the score table—everything.

I'm not sure if it was my desire to show Nowlin I could do it or just nerves about learning in his presence, but I put way too much pressure on myself. His "pointers" were not helping significantly, and I wasn't improving very quickly. That is, until we started in the separate men's and women's leagues. Bowling with a group of women peers wasn't nearly so threatening as feeling like I was the "weak link" on a couples' team where everyone was an experienced bowler.

Many friends of Mike's became friends of ours. By the following May, I had gained confidence and perfected my throw enough to win a trophy in the women's tournament with a score in the 260's while six months pregnant! Maybe if the teaching thing didn't work out....

We were settling into our new life together and making friends. I didn't think about the 20-year-old message from God much anymore. My life had already taken some twists and turns, and though it was very different from anything I'd imagined as a child, Nowlin and I both believed God had brought us together. We loved each other very much and were content to discover our life as a couple with each new set of circumstances, enjoying it or dealing with it as it came.

Just short of our second wedding anniversary, we were blessed with the arrival of our first son, Brian. We were thrilled (and secretly terrified!) at the prospect of being new parents. The questions we hadn't thought to ask in advance ambushed us on a daily basis, and we used our phone-a-friend lifeline more than once.

When Brian was barely two years old, however, our young family experienced one of those heart-wrenching trials. He was a typical toddler going through the "terrible twos" although the only terror was mine—of not being able to keep up with him. He was healthy and full of energy—running, climbing, and jumping everywhere he went. He jabbered and parroted phrases. He laughed and screamed. He giggled and tumbled through every room in the house.

The fun spilled into the outdoors when we let it—under watchful eyes, of course, since we lived a half block from a high school with several hundred teenage drivers coming and going at all hours. Ironically enough, my life, or at least my residential situation, had come full circle back to Will Rogers High School, where I had *not* attended after the move to Bartlesville 15 years earlier and which was right around the corner from the family home Nowlin had inherited after his mother passed away.

Except for the busy corner next to the high school, our neighborhood was quiet, located in a well-established mid-town part of the city, and perfect for raising a family. We were happy there. Brian was a handful and a heartful as well. He was our greatest joy.

One day it dawned on me as evening approached that Brian hadn't been his usual energetic, noisy self. For most of the afternoon since I'd picked him up from the sitter's, he'd been lying on the couch, half-watching the game shows and cartoons on TV instead of running and exploring.

While the passive behavior had allowed me to get more done around the house before Nowlin got home, I was concerned as I realized Brian had become increasingly lethargic over the course of several hours. I felt his forehead and was sure he had a low-grade fever.

Thinking it might be his two-year molars bothering him, I gave him a dose of Tylenol, which seemed to help. He ate a bit of supper, and though he didn't exhibit his normal level of enthusiasm, he did give up the couch that evening and showed some interest in playing with his toys for short periods with Nowlin's prompting. We went to bed hoping he'd be back to normal in the morning.

In the middle of the night, however, we awoke to Brian's whining and moaning. I went to him and could tell that he was burning up. He'd been struggling to get free of the blanket I had tucked around him to protect against the chilly October night. I took his temperature and found his fever had spiked to 105 degrees.

With doctors' offices closed, I wasn't sure where to turn, but Nowlin, who had some experience, though limited, with his daughter from a previous marriage, had the presence of mind to call the hospital emergency room where there were nurses and doctors on duty.

We were told to give Brian Tylenol every four hours regularly, bathe him in tepid water in the bathtub to keep the fever at bay, and call his pediatrician first thing in the morning.

I called in sick early the next day and stayed home to take care of Brian, hoping the substitute would be able to follow my lesson plans and handle the kids at school, who usually had extra energy on Fridays. As soon as the doctor's office was open, I put in the call to the pediatrician and waited for a return call.

Nowlin had gone in to the store but was calling periodically to check on Brian. By mid-morning, Brian had started developing reddish-purple blotches about the size of dimes on his stomach, arms, and legs, in addition to the spikes of high fever and general discomfort that were making him crankier and more listless than ever.

When the doctor's office finally returned the call, I described the newest developments to the doctor himself who told me it was probably chicken pox. He said to continue doing what we were already doing and keep an eye on him. He didn't see any need for us to bring Brian in to the office.

Feeling quite put off by the doctor's nonchalance and sensing that he didn't really know or want to be bothered with trying to find out what was going on, I called the only other person I trusted to give me some insight and advice: my mother. She had raised four children and knew all the signs and symptoms of every childhood disease.

I heard the concern in her voice when she told me that the blotchy rash I had described didn't sound like chicken pox, which in all four of us had manifested itself in watery blisters that accompanied the fever stage. She urged me to call the doctor's office again and insist on getting an appointment or at least some better answers.

The doctor's office never called back, and by evening, after Nowlin got home, when we tried the number we were getting nothing but the weekend answering machine message. We were exhausted, worried, and furious, but that was only the beginning.

Over the weekend, the blotches grew and merged, spreading over Brian's entire body like a stained and faded purplish one-piece pajama. The fever came and went between doses of Tylenol, and he felt so miserable that he didn't want to do anything but sit in my lap. When he wore himself out with fussing and fidgeting and finally fell asleep, I laid him down in his bed, glad for us both to get some rest.

When he woke up from his nap, he was worse. I picked him up out of his bed, and thinking that his squirming and kicking meant he wanted down, I set him on his feet. He fell to the floor. I stood him up again, but as he tried to take the first step, he cried in pain and went to the carpet, his legs buckling under him. He absolutely could not walk, even a step.

We knew we couldn't wait until Monday morning, and by that time neither of us had much confidence in Brian's regular pediatrician anyway. So, Nowlin bundled him up, and we took him to the St. John's Hospital emergency room. The pediatrician on duty that night was another godsend.

Dr. Patrick Daley was attentive and very caring. After listening to our account of the symptoms and behaviors and after giving Brian a preliminary exam, he was at least honest and up-front. He emphatically agreed that it was *not* chicken pox, and although he didn't know exactly what the problem was, he assured us that he would get to the bottom of it. He wanted to admit Brian immediately to the hospital and run a series of tests.

That was the beginning of a long nightmarish week in St. John's, day after day of different kinds of tests. The innumerable blood samples and spinal taps for a multitude of experiments and screenings were surpassed only by the prayers that were offered up for Brian and for the doctors on a daily basis.

Every day on his evening rounds, Dr. Daley would candidly admit, "We still don't really know what we're dealing with, but every day we're eliminating more of the possibilities." I was grateful that he didn't mention names of specific diseases until they had been ruled out. Just hearing the words cancer, scoliosis, polio, cystic fibrosis, and muscular dystrophy was scary enough, even in the same breath that they were dismissed. With every day that passed, we were simultaneously relieved at what it *wasn't* and more uneasy than ever about the possibilities of some rare, little-understood condition that it might be.

Nowlin and I took turns staying with Brian at night, trying to comfort him and take his mind off his pain. Mike and other family members sat with us at the hospital in the evenings, bringing in food, distracting Brian, and running interference for Nowlin at the store when necessary.

During the days, while we were also taking turns missing work, Brian would disappear for hours at a time with one doctor or nurse, then another. Between therapy, rehab, tests, and x-rays, he wasn't in the room with us much except at mealtime and at night.

Sometimes, while Brian was in therapy or having a test run, I would walk through the unit and watch all the chronically and terminally ill children and their parents. Some were somber and sad, others still laughing and trying to make the best of their situation.

I would pray for God to spare us that kind of life, in and out of hospitals, with the constant uncertainty of wondering whether your child was going to live or die. Sorrow at the thought of losing Brian was overwhelming. I prayed and sought God's wisdom, looking for some comfort and a way to face whatever was ahead of us.

I remember thinking that I really wasn't strong enough. If anything happened to Brian, I didn't think I would be able to go on. In those moments, God reminded me of my own grandmother Skidmore who had lost two young children as many mothers had in previous generations when medical knowledge was limited and infant mortality was so high.

God showed me that He carried those parents through and they went on living and even found joy again, though for the first time I understood how none of the joy they felt for other children could possibly have diminished the pain of losing that one particular child.

I was afraid God was preparing me for the worst, so I pleaded for Him to take me instead and spare Brian. In the spiritual exchange that was going on inside my head, God assured me that He knew I was willing to die for Brian, then immediately added, "What if I don't want you, what if I want Brian? Don't you trust me with him? Don't you believe that I also love him, even more than you do?"

With those questions, all my defenses crumbled. I had to admit that God also loved Brian and that even though I didn't understand it or see how I would ever get through it, I had to tell God that He could take my son if that was what He needed to do for His purposes. In the same thought that I trusted God with Brian, I trusted Him to get me through it.

I was desperately searching once again for that safe place inside, that wall to hold me in. Because I wanted to run, and run hard. Not just away from the fear of Brian's death. I believed he would be in heaven with God, waiting for me. The culprit this time was fear of the overwhelming, soul-swallowing sorrow that loomed just beyond his death and of the long lifetime I would have to endure it.

My insides were wrenching in agony not only at the thought of my pain but now at Nowlin's as well. He had already experienced such profound loss and had been through so much tragedy. He'd lost his mother to a fatal shooting accident, on the same night, no less, that his first wife had left with his baby daughter, Carmen, a decade before. He was just beginning to really live again and to allow himself to feel genuine joy.

Then, I pleaded again, this time not for Brian or myself but for Nowlin that God would be merciful and spare him that additional pain. I wasn't sure Nowlin's faith was strong enough to bear this new sorrow, and I feared it might turn him farther away from God instead of bringing him closer.

In the days that followed that exchange with the Lord, Brian began to show signs of improvement. By the next weekend, the doctors still had not come to a diagnosis of what had ailed Brian, but his fever was under better control and his appetite returning. He was beginning to walk again, a few steps at a time, with less and less discomfort.

By the time Dr. Daley released him from the hospital, the best explanation he could give was an "either-or." Either Brian had suffered the onset of juvenile rheumatoid arthritis, or it was a fluke viral infection of the lining of the hip joint socket. In the case of the former, the episodes would recur within a year or two and become progressively worse thereafter. If he never had any more episodes or problems, we could assume after a couple of years that it was the latter case, a strange, one-time viral infection.

For two long years, every time Brian had an ache or a pain or a touch of fever, we prayed that it was only a minor infection, a "bug" going around and not the next episode of JRA. Thankfully, he passed the two-year window and never experienced any of those symptoms again.

What God showed me through that ordeal was that it is easy when you love someone so much to offer yourself to bear the brunt of whatever pain, anguish, or hardship you see that loved one about to endure. That is the nature of true, unselfish love: to value someone else more than you value your own comfort, wellbeing, or even your own life.

The hardest thing to let go of and offer up for sacrifice is not yourself. It is that beloved other, that priceless, cherished loved one who is most precious to you. Yet, that is the extent to which God wants us to trust Him. How much faith does it take to give up something that is not as highly valued? Infinitely greater is the sacrifice of someone who offers up that which is most precious, most prized, and most loved.

That's what Abraham was prepared to give up when he raised the axe against his promised and long-awaited son, Isaac, in obedience to God. That's what God did give up in His own Son, Jesus.

# Home Coming

Mom and Dad had both come from robust family backgrounds. On Dad's side, the Skidmores were well known in the Claremore and Oologah areas through several generations for their honesty, generosity, and hospitality.

My great-grandparents owned the Skidmore ranch referenced in the celebrated play, "Green Grow the Lilacs" by local playwright Lynn Riggs, which became the acclaimed musical production "Oklahoma!" though I'm not sure how accurately or fully their characters were developed in that portrayal.

My grandfather was on the Claremore Police Force for a number of years and later was sheriff of Rogers County. In the law enforcement line of work, his path crossed with many people who were less fortunate. He was wise enough to know that a lot of trouble was born out of desperation and could be avoided by just lending a helping hand when people needed it.

Even through the years of the Great Depression, my grandparents shared whatever they had with whomever was without, opening their home to anyone who needed a hot meal or a place to sleep. There was always good food and good company at the Skidmores' place.

Mom came from a small community a mile or two outside Coalgate, a coal mining town in south central Oklahoma. It became a focal point in the previous century for immigrant families of many nationalities who could always find jobs in the mines when work was scarce for them in the cities. The daughter of a Swedish mother and an Irish father, Mom grew up with much the same set of values as Dad.

A host of medical and some tragic other circumstances, however, hit her family hard, as is often the case in immigrant communities. The influenza pandemic of 1917-18 had claimed the lives of many in her extended family. There were grandparents, aunts and uncles that Mom never knew, as well as cousins who died as infants or children.

Mom's mother was one of six children raised by a widowed father who never remarried after his wife died in childbirth. The family was even more critically important among those who had lost loved ones. Older siblings helped raise younger ones. Aunts and uncles helped raise nieces and nephews. It's what families did.

Both Mom and Dad learned from the same moral code book to work hard, be thankful for what you have, be honest and generous, and respect your fellow man. They learned that people take care of each other and enjoy being together, both in the family and the community.

With their hardy foundation in the love and fellowship of extended families, it was difficult for Mom and Dad to be so isolated in Wichita. Their common history of growing up in the Great Depression dictated that a person went where the job was if he was fortunate enough to find one. He simply made the most of whatever the hardships or inconveniences were. Long past the Depression era, that thinking explained the move to Bartlesville—it wasn't really a personal affront to my 15-year-old existence after all—and later to Kansas.

The folks visited Tulsa on holidays and on weekends in between when they could, or we gathered in Wichita. They kept up with the latest family news through phone calls, cards, and letters.

By this time, my parents had spent 14 years in Wichita, but their brothers, sisters, cousins, and Dad's mother were still here in Oklahoma. Most of my siblings and I, now adults with families of our own, were in the Tulsa area, too.

So, in the summer of 1984, my father retired from Vickers Petroleum Company and my mother from Wichita State University. Our parents, at long last, came back home and settled on the outskirts of Broken Arrow, Oklahoma. It was a bedroom community, part of the greater Tulsa metropolitan area. Everyone was elated, none more than Mom, when she and Dad were finally able to be close by geographically—at least compared to Wichita—and back "in the loop" again.

Their house was on a beautiful corner lot on the south edge of what was then the last housing subdivision between Broken Arrow and Coweta, just off Highway 51. Their back yard shared a fence line with a large vacant acreage which the owners used to pasture horses, a few head of cattle, and an occasional mule.

It was an idyllic setting, the best of both worlds. The beauty and serenity of trees, rolling meadows, and horses grazing were right there outside the dining room window. A few steps farther, through the kitchen door into the garage, the driveway connected with a paved road through the neighborhood all the way to town, only a couple of miles away.

The summer they moved back, Brian was almost three, and I was pregnant with our second child, due in October. With Mom and Dad so near, we relished the summer months and spent as much time as we could together with the extended family during my time off from teaching. Karen and Dubie and their families were nearby, and Ken would drive down often from the City (that's Okie for Oklahoma City) for weekends.

That summer was the beginning of many years of cherished family gatherings in the house on Oakridge Street. On holidays, the long dining table was extended with several leaves to mess hall proportions, with chairs and hungry mouths squeezed in all around. Hardly a square inch of tablecloth could be spotted amid the heaping platters awaiting the blessing. And oh, the Amen clattering of forks and spoons on plates and bowls, harpooning slabs of ham and turkey, dishing up mounds of mashed potatoes and cornbread dressing, and ladling lakes of hot gravy on top!

Not the least of a harvest feast was the colorful array of homegrown vegetables from Dad's garden that garnished every meal: fried okra, yellow squash, cucumbers and onions in vinegar, sliced tomatoes, and freshly snapped green beans cooked to tender perfection. When we thought we couldn't swallow another bite, Mom would ask the eternally bittersweet question, "Who's ready for dessert?" Waist buttons undone and belt holes extended a notch, hardly a man, woman, or child could resist Mom's tantalizing chocolate sheet cake or the melt-in-your-mouth homemade pies.

Cherry, pecan, and coconut cream were the favorites, with cherry-cheese, peach cobbler, and lemon meringue right there in the running. It's no wonder Mom was such a good baker. Pie was a staple in the Harney household while she was growing up. When someone would ask Grandpa, "What kind of pie will you have, Matt?" His pat answer, delivered with a wide grin and a twinkle in his eye, was "Hot or cold!"

As that first summer of '84 drew near its end, the after-dinner conversation would turn inevitably to work topics and the new school year looming ahead. Nowlin and I were still looking for a new babysitter for Brian, one who would also take an infant later in the year. We had checked with a couple of different places and were astounded at how much more they charged for a second child, especially a baby!

We hadn't been hinting or "fishing" for a response. It was a legitimate financial concern and an issue we were still in the process of resolving when soon afterward Mom approached me and offered to keep the kids. I protested at first, not wanting to tie her and Dad down with the responsibility of full-time child care when they should be traveling and enjoying the much-deserved freedom of their retirement years.

But she insisted that she and Dad had already discussed it. Dad had said he would help her, so it wouldn't be too physically demanding. They *wanted* to do it. They were nearby, comparatively speaking, and were looking forward to spending more time with the grandkids, anyway. Plus it would save us a considerable sum of money in child care expenses. It was a win/win situation.

So, Nowlin and I, after making sure they knew what they were taking on—as if they had completely forgotten the ups and downs of raising four children of their own—accepted their generous offer. We were deeply touched and profoundly appreciative. I believe there were a couple of things that had a bearing on their offer though they were left unspoken at the time.

First, the memory of Brian's ordeal in the hospital the year before was still all too fresh in everyone's mind. I had never thought about it from my parents' perspective until now. They must have felt more isolated and helpless than ever, stuck working in Wichita and dependent on phone calls to update them on the precarious condition of a precious grandchild during that long week he was in the hospital. They came as quickly as they could on the weekend, but the waiting and just not being able to be here with us must have been agonizing for them.

Now, not even a full year later, Brian was still in the two-year window, the watch period for further signs and symptoms of Juvenile Rheumatoid Arthritis. Mother must have wondered if a babysitter, or anyone who was not already a friend or family member, would really notice or pay close enough attention to look for the indicators if they did recur.

Second, this was in the aftermath of a highly publicized case of child abduction that had gripped national attention with a perplexing and sinister awakening to the presence of evil among us. Who would watch out for and protect her grandchildren while Nowlin and I were at work, better than she and Dad?

Thus, out of a genuine desire to build a bond with the little ones, to be hands-on and helpful, and also out of a newly engendered mistrust for strangers, even those whose backgrounds and references we thought we had researched, the offer was made and gladly accepted.

The years of driving back and forth across the metro area began. Even so, it felt like home with Mom and Dad a vital part of our everyday lives.

GODSWAY

# Timely Labor

God truly delights in giving us the desires of our heart. Nothing is too miniscule or trivial for Him to notice if we come to Him honestly and in faith. He loves to prove that He is with us in the daily details, not just in the huge decisions and times of hardship.

Several years earlier, as the semester of my student teaching had wound down and I had looked ahead to the job in Dewey I'd already secured for the fall, I had known I would be starting a whole new, perhaps very long, chapter of my employable years doing something I'd felt I was settling for, rather than something I'd been excited about.

The chance encounter with Suzanne Sparks—I know now it was more of a divine appointment—and her offer of a dream-come-true trip to Spain, with other European capitals thrown in as a bonus, had seemed like the perfect pilgrimage for my craft. Just as much, it was the answer to the longing of my heart for something meaningful, exciting, and authentic.

Thus, after borrowing the money for this last "fling" with the exotic before I entered into the practical world of teaching, I had begun my career in education in debt and in over my head.

The assignment in Dewey had gone well enough over all, though for the first few days of school there had been whispers when I walked through the hallway; kids were wondering who the "new girl" was. I'd cut my long hair to a shorter style over the previous summer in a calculated effort to look older, but in every new class I met with, I'd experienced the same efforts by students to hide their shock when they realized I was the teacher and not a new student.

I had enjoyed the robust conversations and challenging questions from those young minds and had even met a couple of students with whom I had music in common. If it had just been teaching Spanish and Latin American Studies and playing my guitar and singing in assemblies when invited, I might have stayed longer than just that first year.

However, attached to the open Spanish Teacher position was also the vacant Cheerleader/Pep Squad Sponsor role. After moving to a new city to begin my own high school years, I had never been in the popular crowd. I'd been introverted and not very social. Even in college, aside from the academic work, I'd concentrated on music and continued my songwriting and my spiritual quest instead of worrying much about a social life. So by the fall of 1974, starting my cheerleader duties was more like Joan Baez standing in for Farah Fawcett than any kind of real fit.

I was never comfortable in the sponsor's role. I had truly tried, from holding practices and hosting fundraisers to chaperoning squad sleepovers, but these were activities I'd never been involved in during my own teenage years. I don't think I did them as much justice as someone with a more outgoing personality might have.

As the year had drawn to an end amid talk of renewing contracts, I had to make a decision. My heart won out over my practicality, and I'd chosen to take a chance and move in a different direction, not knowing exactly where I would be going but certain that it wouldn't be back to the classroom, at least for a while. I hadn't fully understood it at the time, but God knew that adventurous journey to Europe and especially Spain would sustain me through a decade of searching until I found my true niche.

Fast forward through graduate school and romance interrupted, through the franchise in Aurora and the angels on the road, through the happy first years of my new marriage and the trauma with Brian. By now, I had a very close relationship with my God and knew first-hand His faithfulness in *all* situations.

More settled now with a family, for practical and financial reasons, I'd been back in the classroom for several years. Though I saw education as a temporary career, I was good at connecting with children and had settled into it easily enough, trusting that at least for a while this was where God wanted me.

It was more unrealistic than ever to think I could quit teaching and do something different. Even though the pay didn't compare with other professions, it was a steady reliable income, I was good at it, and I loved children. Let's face it, my parents' Depression-era practicality was deeply rooted in me, so my family's financial stability came first. Yet, in those initial years, I always felt like teaching was just my occupation, not my true vocation, my calling. I regretted that the longer I taught beginning Spanish classes year after year, the more I was losing my own fluency and my passion.

After each of our two sons was born I went back to my job teaching Spanish and made the adjustments of juggling school responsibilities with a home, a husband, and first one, then two rambunctious, rough-and-tumble little boys. Depending on Nowlin's schedule, some days he kept the boys at home. Other days, they were at Mom and Dad's. When my work day finished, I rushed home to hear recounts from the other adults of Brian's latest antics and what new word our second son, Bret, had learned.

There's an early video of Nowlin giving Bret a banana and then coaxing out of him the adorable answer "balana" to his daddy's repeated questions about what he was eating. All the while, he sat inside an open cabinet with feet hanging out among pots and pans strewn all over the kitchen floor. It could probably have won a spot on the hit show "America's Funniest Home Videos" a few years later if I'd had the time or thought to submit it.

My dad got the biggest kick out of letting Bret 'help' him mow the lawn. Dad would stretch his arms out full length as he pushed so that Bret could walk between him and the mower, holding onto a lower bar on the handle. That soon spawned a prolonged obsession with all things lawn related—and a special aversion to them by the time he was a teenager!

Bret would look at the ads in newspapers and magazines with Mom, repeating in toddler-ese the name of every lawn tool they could find and cut out: "lawn-lawn" for lawn mower, "dimmy" for trimmer, "weedeedy" for weed eater, and "bigalo" for the trickier sprinkler. He was the only almost-two-year-old I had ever known with an identified hobby and scrapbook to go with it and most certainly the only 3-year-old who requested a lawn mower on his birthday cake!

I had always thought I wanted three children, but since Carmen was living with us at that time, I supposed I had my three and questioned whether I was up to another infant anyway. Our family was like so many others, a blend of full and step siblings, with gaps in age groups, and we worked hard to make each child feel loved and valued as a unique part of the family unit.

My middle-school-aged stepdaughter loved her little brothers and though at times reluctant, she was very good help with them. I loved them all dearly, and there was never a doubt they were all worth the time and energy. I'll admit, though, that having teenagers and toddlers in the house at the same time was tricky.

I loved working with children, but I looked forward to weekends, holidays, and especially summers with my own kids. I was almost jealous of every hour I had to spend away from them. We were not a perfect family, and there was some 'baggage' from the past, but we tried to learn from it and provide the best home we could. Regardless of everything else, it was always a labor of love.

When childhood diseases would spread through the Kindergarten class and through the family, the doctor visits and medicines came out of our pocket and budget since the high deductibles somehow never allowed our insurance plan to kick in and pay for the services. Even with both parents working, at jobs that paid too little, there was rarely much money left over at the end of the month when all the bills were paid.

Being a teacher, with lessons to plan and papers to grade, often at home, my time and energy were always stretched thin and at a premium. I began to feel "locked in" as to my career choice, but I was determined to persevere, making it as interesting and fun as I could for my students and myself.

When pregnancy number three slipped up on us unexpectedly, Nowlin and I were both flooded with mixed emotions. How would we manage financially, not just with medical and hospital bills but also with fitting another full-time, long-term member of the family into the already-tight budget? What if I didn't have enough stamina and patience to give a new baby the care and quality time it deserved?

And...*what if it's another boy*??? The very thought sent me into overload! I had always wanted a daughter of my own. I loved Carmen dearly, and I knew that our mostly-stable home was a much-needed influence in her life. But she was nine years old (going on 30!) when she came to live with us, and I had missed out on those early little-girl years.

So, I warmed quickly to the idea of a baby girl, thinking of the frilly dresses and the fun fixing her hair in cute girlie-girl pigtails. We'd bake cookies together and have tea parties...

But *WHAT IF IT'S ANOTHER BOY*??!! I was trying to adjust and even look forward to the new addition, but God is my witness, every time I thought of having another boy I went into an inward, private panic. It wasn't that I didn't love my sons. I did. Brian and Bret meant more to me than I could ever express! It wasn't that I wanted to change them. Every ounce of energy and every little quirk made them who they were and made them each individually whom I loved so much.

Still, something in me knew this would be my last baby. I already understood what it was like to have boys. I wanted to experience the baby-girl thing. I wanted the boys to have a sister closer to their age to grow up with. I wanted the calming and balancing effect it would bring to the family. I wanted that special mother-daughter bond, like the one I had with my own mother. I wanted to pass the nurturing, the recipes, and the heritage of the strong, hard-working, loving women in my family on to the next generation.

So, I began to pray. I prayed that God would give me peace of mind and help me rise to the challenge, to find the energy and the joy for whatever lay ahead. I would always end my prayer with, *"Please, Lord, you know the desire of my heart. I'll love any child you bless me with, but please, if possible, according to Your will, let it be a baby girl."*

As the pregnancy advanced, there were recently-developed tests and cutting edge procedures that my new doctor wanted to perform. I had ditched my private practice doctor when he dallied so long getting to the hospital that even after a 15-hour labor, Bret was delivered by the anesthesiologist.

My new doctor was one of five in a group practice. The shared expenses allowed them to have more up-to-date equipment. One of the tests Dr. West encouraged was amniocentesis, a new procedure to extract, via an 8-inch needle, amniotic fluid to test for birth defects, Downs Syndrome, or other abnormalities. There was also now a way to know the gender of the fetus through ultrasound imaging.

At age 35, those tests were mandatory. Since I was still 34, he would leave it up to Nowlin and me to decide. We talked it over and came to the conclusion that we didn't want to know in advance.

What if something were wrong, would we spend the rest of the pregnancy worrying and dreading the birth of our own child? God forbid! So, we passed on the testing for birth defects, and we passed on knowing the sex of the baby. Better just to do it the old fashioned way, by faith. So, my prayers now were two dimensional, "Please God, let it be a healthy, normal baby girl."

In the spring of 1986, as the school year and my second trimester were both coming to a close amid not-really-so-clever jokes among my teacher friends like, "Don't you know not to drink the water in Mexico?" I got some disheartening news. The Spanish program was being cut at Carver Middle School.

In an economic downturn, the state and local district were experiencing a financial shortfall. They were eliminating some programs and not renewing contracts for many first year teachers. Although I was a tenured teacher by then and not in jeopardy of losing my job, I was in a "non-essential" program and was being "trimmed" from my current assignment.

I would be starting with a completely different program, the ESL (English as a Second Language) Center in an entirely unfamiliar building on the other side of town the next fall. Instead of teaching Spanish to English-speaking students, I would be doing exactly the opposite, teaching English to immigrant children whose first languages were from all over the globe.

How could I do that?! The only language I spoke fluently, besides English, was Spanish, with a brief exposure to French many years before during my first semester in college and some partially forgotten Portuguese from graduate school in Fayetteville. I tried not to think about how I would even begin to tackle this latest, seemingly impossible, teaching assignment.

In addition, with my due date late in August, the 26th, it was going to be tricky enough to navigate the beginning of the school year and the simultaneous start of my maternity leave. Even with familiar people, surroundings, and curriculum it would be difficult, and much more so with all the uncertainty of an entirely new assignment.

What if I were in the hospital on the mandatory teacher-report date? What if this baby were late, like both of her older brothers? I'd be in my new position only for a week or two, and then the students would have a substitute for the rest of the nine weeks. So, I prayed, *"Lord, let this be a healthy baby girl, and let her come not too soon so I won't have to miss the first day to report to my new post. And let her not be too late so these immigrant children won't have an extra teacher-change to adjust to."*

Beyond the start of school and the impending maternity leave, I was too preoccupied and excited about the coming birth itself to mull or stew any longer about what my new assignment in the ESL Center would be like. I would worry about that when the time came.

However, deep inside, apart from the predominant aspects and immediacy of my pregnancy, something was nudging that sleeping spirit of adventure. In those brief moments when my curiosity went beyond the maternity leave to envision myself in that global classroom, there was a feeling of excitement. I sensed something important just around the corner, and I knew the change would be good.

As the summer wore on and I got more uncomfortable, many of the unpleasant details of my other pregnancies came vividly back to me. The 2½ long weeks past the due date with Brian, before the end of which I was sure they would have to hoist me to the hospital in a crane. The long 18-hour first-child labor, during which every blood vessel in my face popped, leaving me for another week after delivery with a whole crop of tiny blood-red "freckles." Bret was only slightly better at 15 hours and only one week overdue. Now, I was really praying, for very selfish reasons, *"Lord, let this be a healthy baby girl. Let her come on time, and come quickly and easily."*

By mid-August, with the big day looming near, Dr. West began prepping me on what the procedure would be. When I went into labor, I was to call the regular office number even if it was after hours or on a weekend. The answering service would relay the message to whichever doctor was on call, and he would meet me at the hospital.

*Wait. What? Whichever doctor was on call??!!* I hadn't even thought of the possibility that it wouldn't be Dr. West. The surprise must have shown on my face. He reassured me it was common practice. They all had access to the same information, and all covered for each other. It would be fine. All five were well-qualified, experienced doctors. Well, it would *not* be fine with *me*! I had not changed doctors and spent the last eight months getting to know and trust the new one only to have this baby also delivered by a total stranger!!

During those last weeks, I came to know the meaning of that scriptural phrase, "Pray without ceasing." While I went on with the daily routines and the normal preparations for the new arrival, every pause in my day, every silent moment was filled with this prayer, *"Lord, please let this be a healthy baby girl. Please let her come on time, and let the labor be short. And please, please, Lord, let Dr. West deliver my baby."*

Shortly after midnight on August 26th, my water broke. Nowlin made the call to the doctor's office, left a message with the answering service, and then hurried me to St. John's Hospital, where just over an hour later none other than Dr. West met us. At 2:19 A.M. the most beautiful, healthy baby girl I had ever seen burst into the world and was laid on my chest. Nowlin and I both beamed with joy amid tears of relief and thanksgiving.

I was awed at the precision with which God had answered my detailed prayers. There she was, our Cara Beth, a *healthy* baby *girl*, born *on* her due date, after a mere *two-hour* labor, and delivered by *our own doctor*, who of a group of five doctors, just "happened" to be on call. The odds would be against more than a few of those specific details coming true, but with God, all things are possible!

I had reported on the mandatory teachers' first day and met the staff at the ESL Center. Headed by the Team Leader, a fascinating Chinese woman, Dr. Hsu, they were a warm, interesting group of educators who all made me feel welcome and wished me well with the baby. Then, only a couple of days later, I was in the hospital having Cara before the students even started class.

During those precious first weeks of bonding with my new daughter, I marveled at God's goodness and was overwhelmed not only with the joy of this precious gift of a child but also at the spectacular display of His perfect timing and precise orchestration of the details surrounding her birth, about which I had prayed so arduously.

That was just the obvious miracle. When the leave was over, and I was forced to tear myself away from the full time care of that little angel, I gathered my strength and returned to the classroom for my next challenge.

The combined group of fourth and fifth graders was huge and was composed of students from almost every continent on the planet. They spoke a dozen different languages and for the most part stared in silence when I spoke English.

It was overwhelming and chaotic at times. As the weeks passed, I learned the techniques of using visual cues, modeling language, and acting out meaning. As I discovered the individual histories of those students, some frightening, some tragic—all traumatic in some way—they absolutely captured my heart.

There was a boy from war-torn El Salvador. He could never seem to sit still or relax after so many anxious years of hiding from gunmen in the streets and hearing their bullets blazing in spurts nearby.

There were several children from Vietnam, like the little girl who had arrived here straight from a refugee camp. At lunch, she would lower her head to tray level, scoop a bite into her mouth with her fingers while peering around the table, and seem to wonder why no one was fighting her for the food. Another child would drop to the floor at the sound of an airplane passing overhead and hide under his desk until the roar of its engine was out of ear shot. There was also the boy who had fallen out of the boat during the escape with his family from Vietnam, who apparently suffered permanent effects from almost drowning.

One Spanish-speaking boy had inadvertently walked in on and witnessed a sexual crime being committed. For a while, he acted out his trauma with suggestive and inappropriate gestures and movements, disrupting and disturbing the other students.

A girl from Liberia had been separated from her family and sent here to get a better education and to learn English. She was homesick, angry and often uncooperative.

A boy from another African nation in a similar situation would roll on the floor and throw tantrums on occasion from sheer frustration at not being able to communicate or cope with his new surroundings.

It became apparent very quickly that these children needed much more than English or any language for that matter. I could communicate with the Spanish-speaking parents directly and was able to help more readily with their children's adjustment and their families' establishment in the community. I understood their non-educational needs more easily and directed them to charities and other agencies that could help them.

It was a slower process for the children whose first languages were not represented among our faculty. I realized after just a few short weeks that what these children needed more than anything else was love, stability, and time to heal. So, I began to pray for this new group of troubled children, that God would give me patience, insight, and wisdom to know what they needed and how to provide it.

Over time, they warmed to me. In broken English, they began to open up about their pasts, their present circumstances, and eventually, their dreams. The tears and tantrums gave way to wide grins, laughter, and singing.

We drew, gestured, and pantomimed our way into new understanding. We played games, using real-life props to enhance comprehension. We wrote and illustrated stories about actual experiences. We built, created, chanted, memorized, and recited.

Learning from each other about our various cultures, we sang and danced and acted out plays celebrating our differences and performed for audiences of grateful, weepy-eyed parents at Thanksgiving, Christmas, and Chinese New Year.

In learning about the seasons, we cleaned the playground and nearby park on Earth Day and danced around a May pole to welcome spring. We moved from food and gardening into a spring weather unit (common in Oklahoma because of the frequency of tornadoes) using pictures to identify the aspects of certain weather events.

One day, wanting to access students' prior experience, I asked if anyone had seen or been in a tornado. One student, while attempting to tell us about his family's close call, made the innocent substitution of the familiar and similar-sounding word *tomato* for *tornado*. When I illustrated the two scenarios on the board, of a giant tornado almost hitting a house and then a giant tomato almost hitting the same house, there was uproarious laughter.

We laughed at ourselves for our mis-speaks in English—because everyone made them—having fun, not making fun, with every new challenge. We were immersed in real communication. These children were coming back to life, feeling love again, and experiencing, some for the first time ever, true joy and hope.

After my first year with ESL, in the Fall of 1987, at one of the initial staff meetings, the district director who oversaw the ESL services informed Dr. Hsu and me that the Spanish program had been reinstated at Carver Middle School where I had been before. Although they would be sorry to see me leave the Center, she wanted me to have the first option of going back to Carver if I wanted to before they advertised for a new Spanish teacher.

I didn't even have to think about it. My immediate response was gratitude for the offer but an adamant no! These families had touched my heartstrings, and I was invested now. I remained with the ESL program for over 20 years; in that time, I was blessed to know and serve hundreds of very special students and families from around the world.

My fluency and vocabulary in Spanish grew and became better than ever before, and each new school year was a highly anticipated adventure not just in teaching but in really making a difference in people's lives.

It was only in retrospect as I mused years later over that first year at the ESL Center and the whole new world it opened up for me that I realized it was a year of double blessing. In addition to Cara's arrival, about which I'd been very vocal, God had also answered a prayer I'd never really prayed. He'd responded to my deep inner desire to use my Spanish skills for something real, important, and bigger than myself. He had shown me my true calling.

I'd been so exhilarated at the time by the miracle of specific answered prayers surrounding the labor and delivery of my baby daughter, I hadn't seen then that God had also known the unexpressed, hidden desire of my heart, nearly forgotten by me but not by Him. It would not be the last time in my life He responded to a long-forgotten need.

The realization shouldn't have surprised me so much. After all, "He that spared not His own Son, but delivered Him up for us all, how shall He not with Him also freely give us all things?" (Romans 8:32) God knew all along my logistical needs and my heartfelt desires in both situations: my daughter's birth and my new job. As I dared to commit the details to Him in prayer and trust Him, He smiled in response and worked out every precise answer to every spoken and hidden request in this very timely labor.

# Hearts Rerouted

For several years until the kids were school age, minus the spans of maternity leave, I would rise early, gather kids, car seats, and diaper bags packed the night before and make the trek to Broken Arrow to drop off the beloved cargo. I'd pray that traffic wasn't too slow on the Broken Arrow Expressway and make my way, sometimes at a crawl, more than 15 miles back across the metro area to work. For a few years, I was at Carver Middle School at Cincinnati and Greenwood, where I taught Spanish. Later, I reported to Byrd Middle School where the ESL Center was housed.

Depending on our specific work situation each year, sometimes Nowlin would take the kids and I would pick them up. Other times, I would do morning, and he'd pick up in the evening. The daily jaunts were well worth the time and gasoline, however, in exchange for the peace of mind and the flourishing relationships between grandparents and grandchildren.

Even considering the near-disaster when Bret was a toddler and fell against the brick edge of the fireplace before Mom could free her hands and follow him out of the kitchen, the benefits outweighed the negatives. That fall only required a few stitches to the forehead, and as active as he was, it could have happened just as easily at home with us.

Nowlin and I would listen to play-by-play accounts of the first-time events Mom and Dad felt blessed to witness. They would tell stories, not just to us but to any relatives or other visitors, about too-cute words and phrases the kids came up with in the course of their make-believe play.

Like the time they went pretend fishing out the back of dad's pickup, parked in the garage where the adults were cleaning and organizing storage closets. When mom asked them if they caught anything, Bret replied enthusiastically "I caught a catfish!" Cara, about three years old at the time, tried to one-up her brother by declaring "And I caught a dogfish!" Mom and Dad howled every time they retold that story. There was no doubt in anyone's mind, the sun rose and set each day in those grandkids.

Then, one weekend late in the summer of 1989, we got a call from Dubie on a Saturday evening, saying that Dad had called her from the Broken Arrow Hospital where he had taken Mom. She hadn't been feeling well, her arm was aching, and she had a heavy, uncomfortable feeling in her chest. Dr. McBride was meeting them at the ER. That was all that needed to be said, Nowlin and I were on our way.

We sat in the waiting room with Dubie and her husband Oman while the doctors ran tests. My sister filled me in on the events leading up to the ER.

On Friday, she'd been to see Mom and Dad. Mom had told her then about the pain in her right arm that hit her when she was vacuuming. She empathized with the pain Dubie had suffered in the muscle tissue of her arms, which was later called fibromyalgia. She told Mom to check with the doctor about it the next week if it didn't go away.

On Saturday, Mom still was not feeling well, but she was never one to give in to a little pain or discomfort. She and Dad had arranged to go see Grandma Skidmore in Claremore and do some work in her yard. There'd been a storm that did some damage to the trees, and Dad needed to cut broken limbs and chop the biggest pieces into fire wood. So, the plans went forward at Mom's insistence.

While Dad was doing the clean-up and loading the wood into his pickup, Mom was inside with Grandma. She had leaned her head back against the padded armchair to try and relax and get comfortable. But as the hours passed, Grandma could tell Mom was feeling worse. The pain in her arm had not gone away, and the heavy feeling in her chest would not subside. Mom described a foaminess in her mouth now, and though she was not in any kind of excruciating pain, she "just couldn't get comfortable."

Finally, Grandma, still very alert and agile in spite of her 90-plus years, was so worried, God bless her, that she went outside and told Dad she was concerned about Carrie and thought he ought to get her to the doctor right away. The yard work would wait.

Dad loaded up the last log or two and went inside to check on Mom. Though Mom protested that she didn't think it was anything serious, Dad agreed with Grandma and said they would go home and call the doctor.

Thirty minutes later, from her home phone, Mother described her symptoms to Dr. McBride who insisted on meeting them at the hospital. Mom added apologetically, "I hope I'm not sending you on a wild goose chase," to which he replied good naturedly, "Let's hope you *are*! But let's check it out anyway."

My Dad, who was often laughing and acting silly in the privacy of his own home with family around, had a more reserved and stoic presence in public, especially under crisis. He was usually the calm in the midst of the storm, a demeanor he had perfected during his years serving in the military in WWII. He was accustomed to controlling his emotions and letting down his guard only when *he* chose to.

When he'd tried to explain to my sister on the phone what was happening, however, he was so overcome with emotion that Dubie couldn't fully understand what he was trying to say. She heard something about "hospital" and "mother." "You mean your mother, Grandma, is in the hospital?" she asked for clarification, knowing where they had spent the day. Dad pulled it together enough to make the correction, "No, *your* mother!"

His beloved Carrie, his "bride of 46 years"— the number went up annually as he continued to describe her in that manner for almost six decades—had suffered a broken arm from slipping on the icy pavement in Wichita one winter. She'd had a few colds and stomach viruses through the years but had generally been so healthy that nothing had ever threatened to take her away from him. Until now. The initial blood work showed a high level of an enzyme that indicated she had had a heart attack.

Now, in one simple blood test, the news of heart disease and a major heart attack had threatened the love of Dad's life and shattered the secure world they had been so careful and so grateful to build together. He could hardly get the words out to Dubie on the phone.

By the time we all arrived at the hospital, he was more composed, though still worried, and was waiting to hear from the doctor what would happen next. Finally, the white coat emerged from behind private doors and explained that Mom would be taken to Saint Francis Hospital in Tulsa where they would do an angiogram to determine the location and severity of the blockage that had caused the heart attack. That test would tell us the next step, whether the less invasive angioplasty would suffice or if a bypass surgery would be necessary. The prayers started rising on the spot.

The next afternoon, the results of the angiogram showed two places of special concern. One blood vessel was 70% blocked, and the other over 90% blocked. The heart specialist would be performing the angioplasty procedure the following morning. The doctor also explained in advance that if for any reason it became clear that the procedure was not working, they would be prepared to do immediate bypass surgery.

We were stunned. Those were not the results we had been praying for. Mom was going in for what could be major heart surgery tomorrow! What if something...I couldn't finish the thought. I agreed to call Karen and tell her the news. Dubie would call Ken.

I knew we were all praying, but in my private meditations, I implored for, and at the same time wondered if I dared request, a miracle. God had already done so many extraordinary things for me! I wondered if I were pushing the limits by crying out for something so huge as an actual healing.

Then, He brought a young woman from Bartlesville to mind who had attended the same high school Kenny and I had. She had also been active in the Believers Fellowship church in Stillwater. After she graduated from OSU, the young woman had gotten married only to be diagnosed with ovarian cancer within the first year of her marriage. I had joined the whole BF fellowship in praying for her to be healed. A few weeks later, when she went back to her doctor to begin treatments, the doctors could find no cancer. She had been miraculously cured. (Full disclosure: recent communications with some who knew her indicate the cancer may have returned at a later time and taken her.)

God reminded me of all the times He had protected me in my travels and of the incredible precision with which He had answered my many specific prayers when Cara was born. That evening, in an urging from the Spirit, I called both sisters, using a new feature on our phone system called conference call. What better time to try it out? My sisters and I needed to be agreeing together in prayer for Mom.

We prayed, thanking God for His watchful care over Mom and Dad, thanking Him for the mighty work He was going to do and the marvelous way He was going to use these circumstances to build people's faith and to glorify Himself. We called up scripture and claimed the promises of God for our loved ones.

After 10-15 minutes, the peace of God settled in us, and we said good night and hung up, to continue our private supplications. I was filled with an unspeakable joy, almost anticipation. I knew God was going to do an extraordinary work. I didn't know what He had planned, but I knew it was something big.

The next day I stayed within feet of the telephone. I couldn't very well take small children to the hospital, so Dubie would be there with Dad and call me when the procedure was done. Nowlin went on to work only when I insisted that I would call him the minute I heard something.

Out of the convenience store business and now in realty, he and a partner had opened a new business, Buyers' Realty, and he had some paperwork to line up for a house deal that was closing. There was nothing he could do for anyone by staying at home. It was just a matter of waiting now. So, he agreed, and I promised to call him as soon as I heard from anyone, hopefully before noon.

The call came much earlier than I anticipated. My sister's voice was incredulous as she blurted out, "Diana, you're not gonna believe this. They didn't have to do the procedure or the surgery!" My mind was racing through possible explanations. Did they have a conflict of schedule?

Another emergency? Did something happen to the doctor, or worse, to Mom??

"Wh...what do you mean?" I managed to stammer back. She said the doctors returned shortly after they'd taken Mom to the O.R. They had done another angiogram before they started the procedure, to confirm exactly where the blockages were. They were shocked. They couldn't explain why, but there was no longer any obstruction anywhere.

The blood flow had rerouted itself through other vessels, utilizing smaller capillaries around the blocked area, and the heart was now pumping blood normally again, unrestricted. *None of the doctors had ever seen anything like it!* They confirmed in amazement that Mom's heart had literally, overnight, done its own bypass. No need for angioplasty, much less open-heart surgery. She was perfectly fine!

Dubie described being overcome herself as Dad wept openly for joy at the news. God was mightily praised and glorified that day. I know the Lord healed the circulation of blood through Mom's heart. He also used that miracle to reroute the journeys of faith and clear some road blocks, forging a new course for all who witnessed it: doctors, family, husband, parents, children, and grandchildren. Praise God for His mighty works! And He was only getting started.

# Failed Brakes

I wanted to continue the momentum of the faith-building miracle around Mom's heart. As a mother of young children, I wanted not only to love them and take care of them but also to foster in them an awareness of spiritual things and a desire to know God. I wanted them to know Him and trust Him as I did. I didn't want them to experience the fear and unsureness I had, so I began to pray for opportunities to demonstrate walking by faith to them.

I was aware by this time of the decades of confusion and uncertainty my dad had experienced in his faith journey, trying to reconcile the difference between those who were hypocrites but had "a form of godliness" and those who truly sought God and lived a life of faith. I didn't want to be a hypocrite. I didn't want that confusion for my own children.

I wanted them to learn to seek God in a personal way for their own needs. I wanted them to understand that He hears each one of their unique, individual prayers. I didn't want them to just echo what they had heard in Sunday school and church during periods when we were attending here and there as a family. I didn't want to leave them to wonder or have to figure it all out on their own, either. There would be enough they had to learn personally through experience.

I wanted them to have some concrete examples to look back on of people, like me, standing on faith, praying and seeking God, talking to Him as a friend and heavenly Father, and witnessing His response. I looked for opportunities in my everyday life to show them my faith, and God obliged.

School Teacher was about the lowest rung on the professional career ladder in Oklahoma, so I was not raking in big bucks. For many of his working years, Nowlin was self-employed, so there were periods when it was touch-and-go financially. Especially once the kids started coming along, we were always on a modest budget and were glad just to, usually, make ends meet.

With both of us working outside the home, however, we needed two cars. Pre-children, we'd driven some brand new cars. Nowlin had bought the Ranchero, and our first vehicle purchased together as a married couple was a very cool 1979 Pontiac Firebird Trans Am—we're talking Smokey and the Bandit cool—with T-top and everything.

After the Trans Am was irreparably damaged in a hail storm—what a heartbreak!—we had to get more practical in its replacement. So, while the kids were growing up, we drove mostly used cars that were in good shape.

My teaching assignment at the ESL Center was in a building across town from where we lived then. The neighborhood school near our house didn't have a daycare, so when Brian got old enough to enroll in Kindergarten, the year after Cara was born, we enrolled him in Jonas Salk Elementary. I had scoped it out in preparation.

Salk shared an adjacent parking lot with the Byrd Middle School building where the ESL Center was housed, and it had a daycare at one end of the building. Kindergarten was still just half-days then, which made it difficult for working mothers. Salk would be perfect since Brian's teacher would walk the group staying for childcare down to their room after school. Plus, I could walk across a parking lot to get him and take him back to my classroom if I still had work to do.

It worked out so well that when Bret and Cara were old enough we enrolled them at Salk, too. Since my school hours and location and the kids' were so similar, I started doing all the hauling, in a second-hand blue and white GMC Trey Tech van. The up-side of having the kids close to where I worked was that we didn't have to worry about them being unsupervised for long periods in the afternoon while waiting for me to pick them up. The down-side was that I had to cart a van full of little ones back and forth across town every day on the expressway.

One morning, when the kids were all still in grade school at Salk, we were en route, making the daily pilgrimage. Trying to beat the "tardy bell," we were about to take the usual Sheridan exit off the highway. I braked to slow down as we turned onto the exit ramp, but nothing happened. I hit the brakes hard again and still no response. My foot went all the way to the floor.

My first reaction—just for a split second—was panic, but remembering my recent prayers, I quickly realized that with the kids watching, God wanted me to show them my faith, not my fear. Reminded of the other close encounters I'd had on the highway, I began to pray, out loud for their sakes, knowing that God was going to do something amazing.

I don't remember the exact words I prayed, but I remember thanking God for his loving protection and acknowledging that I couldn't stop the van but knew He could. I prayed that He would guide us away from other traffic, and not let us be harmed nor harm anyone else.

While I was talking out loud to God, still pumping the brakes to no avail, we were quickly approaching a line of cars already stopped at a red light at the bottom of the ramp where we would normally have turned right. I could see that at the speed we were going, we would hit the line of cars in our lane before they could all turn, even if the light had already been green.

I swerved into the left-turn lane which was empty, still trying the brakes repeatedly, and prayed as we approached the bottom that the light would change and stop traffic in the main street so that I wouldn't plow into someone as I barreled through the intersection.

At the bottom of the ramp, only a few feet from where I needed to stop, the brakes suddenly grabbed, and given one last firm stomp on the pedal, the van jolted to rest just before going into the oncoming morning traffic.

I sat there numb for a few moments, still processing all that had happened in those brief seconds, and marveling at the persistent way in which God continued to protect us. Our light turned green, and after waiting for the cars in the right lane to make their turns, I was able to pull over behind them and also turn in the direction we needed to go.

We proceeded on our way to school with no further hint of brake problems. We thanked God out loud the whole last mile and a half for answering our prayers, for stopping the van, and for keeping us safe. And silently, I thanked God for demonstrating in such a mighty way to my children His wondrous love and protection. Though they were young, they were old enough to learn a lesson about prayer and about faith in a good and loving God.

# The New Year Kindling

The first waking minutes of that sunny, crisp Saturday morning, January 2, 1999, gave no clue to the eternal significance their following hours would spawn. I'd spent most of the previous week recovering from the latest bout of chronic bronchitis but was finally feeling better.

The first sound was the soft crackle of plastic as my foot swung out from the covers and landed on the stack of folded shopping bags left over from the holidays, still waiting to be put in the re-use bin. With Christmas vacation drawing to a close, I was feeling depressed at not having accomplished more around the house during that second week.

On Monday, we would resume the hectic back-and-forth schedule of school and sports. There were practices and games for the boys' two different basketball teams and Cara's pom squad. So much of my time was spent chauffeuring kids, who were now in middle and high school, aside from my own teaching responsibilities, that I felt frazzled all the time and spread way too thin. I was not looking forward to the long stretch of weeks until Spring Break, but for the first time in days, I woke feeling normal, almost 100% recovered.

It was going to be a great day, starting with a few hours of much anticipated Grandma duty, to end the holidays on a bright note. Carmen, now married with several young children of her own, had a mandatory store meeting at Arby's, and our son-in-law would already be at work. So, I had agreed to watch the grandkids for a couple of hours.

Bret had spent Friday night at "uncle" Mike's, as the kids had grown up calling him. They were to pick up Nowlin and go to watch Brian play an early basketball game across town.

I calculated that Cara, now 12 years old and starting to acquire some teenage sleeping habits, would still be in bed sawing logs when I got back from Carmen's by mid-morning. If she did wake up, she was certainly old enough to get herself some cereal and watch T.V. for a short while until I returned.

So, I left Cara asleep and Nowlin getting ready for the ball game. It wasn't what I witnessed but what I missed in the interim between my leaving home and the knock on Carmen's door that was life-changing.

Mike's role as family friend had deepened and grown into much more than that since the early years in the 7-Eleven store. Though from a large family, his own life had been shaped by early loss and then by caring for his mother and had not resulted in a wife and children of his own, in spite of the family-man type that he was.

Through the years, his clan and ours intermingled, Mike embracing our parents, siblings, nieces, and nephews, and Nowlin and I visiting and celebrating with his as well. We mourned with him when Mama Lu passed, and he reciprocated when any of our extended family suffered a hardship or the loss of a loved one.

Our kids were the family he would never have, and he treated them like they were his own, showering them with his generous spirit, his wisdom, his time and support, as well as every new trinket or technology their hearts could desire. He also enforced discipline and held them to high moral and ethical standards, including punctuality, as a true mentor and role model should. If he said he would pick them up at a certain time, he was always there 15 minutes early. If they weren't close enough to being ready, he wasn't inclined to wait for very long, or so he convinced them.

It was a common thing for the kids to spend a Friday night at Mike's because he was always more fun than we parents! He would take them to movies, concerts, and even a professional wrestling smack down one time. Sometimes, they'd browse the record and video game shops in the mall, and he always had a knack for finding bargains on the latest fad in sneakers or jeans, or yes, hair bows and purses for Cara. Mom used to say, quite affectionately, "Every family needs an Uncle Mike!" He truly changed our definition of family.

As Nowlin tells the story of that post-New Year morning, Mike and Bret were supposed to come by for him at 9:00 a.m. Brian, now driving, was long gone to be on time for pre-game team meeting and warm-up. The varsity tip off was at 10:00, but the guys wanted to leave early enough to get good seats at the high school where it was being played, which was on the other side of downtown.

Nowlin showered and dressed, then went into Cara's room to let her know he was getting ready to leave. He kissed her on the forehead and reminded her that I was at Carmen's but would be back in an hour or two. She mumbled some sleepy acknowledgement but didn't fully awaken.

He sat for a while in the living room sipping his coffee and waiting for Mike. Nine o'clock came and went. He looked through the reflection of the Christmas tree in the front picture window and started to get antsy, thinking their chances of getting good seats were fading. Where could Mike be? He was *never* late. Of all days!

All of a sudden, Nowlin got a whiff of a strong foul odor, like rubber burning. He darted to the kitchen thinking I must have left a burner on, but no, there was nothing cooking. He scampered through the back porch down to the boys' bedroom, converted from the garage. They must have left something too close to the portable radiator. But again, all seemed fine.

By the time he ran back to the living room, in just a matter of seconds, the recently installed smoke alarm went off in the hallway on the other end of the house between Cara's room and ours. He opened our bedroom door, hardly registering the hot handle, and was shocked at what he saw.

He said it was surreal, like a scene from a movie. The east wall behind our bed was on fire. Flames were dripping down from the ceiling onto the bed, and the covers and curtains were igniting faster than he could think.

For a split second, he wondered if he should get some water and try... then, a voice told him emphatically, *"No! This is more than you can handle."* So, he burst into Cara's room, shouting "Cara! Fire! Get up! Don't stop to grab anything; you don't have time to get dressed. Just get out the front door, NOW! I'll meet you in the front yard."

Cara, hearing the frantic tone of voice and seeing the smoke filling the hallway, grabbed her kitty and obediently dashed out the front in just her night shirt, legs bare from the knees down, and arms under short sleeves at the mercy of the frosty January morning.

Meanwhile, Nowlin sped to the back porch and threw open the door to the yard, tossing Boots, the family dog, outside, practically all in one motion. He raced to the kitchen, jerked the receiver off the wall phone, and dialed 911. "Fire! 3731 E. 4th Street. Hurry!" He left the phone still dangling on the cord as he rushed back through the living room, toward the front door.

Before he could get outside, Smokey, Cara's cat (named for her gray coat long before the fire!) dashed back inside from the front yard and headed straight toward the burning bedroom!

Nowlin, to this day, doesn't know how he moved fast enough, but as she streaked by him, he thrust his arm back and down and managed to grab her up by the scruff of her neck. He took a few steps toward the hall and slammed the door shut between the living room and hallway in case she tried to get back inside again, then sprinted out to meet Cara in the yard, with Smokey tightly tucked under one arm.

Cara was shivering and scared, very relieved to see her daddy coming safely out of the house with Smokey in tow. Nowlin hustled her toward the house across the street, where they could stay warm while waiting for the fire truck. As they reached the curb, they saw Mike's car coming up over the hill.

Of course, I knew nothing of the fire until Nowlin called me and, almost simultaneously, Mike and Cara showed up at Carmen's. When the phone rang, still before cell phones, I didn't answer it, at first, since it wasn't my home, but it quit ringing only for a few seconds and then began again.

I sensed an urgency and finally picked it up. Nowlin's voice was strained but calm while assuring me that everyone was fine, but we had had a fire. I immediately pictured a burning skillet, thinking he had fixed something for himself after I left. I asked if he'd found the baking soda and gotten it put out. His slow deliberate beginning, "NO, you don't understand..." let me know something was seriously wrong even before his words finished, "We had a *house* fire!"

My mind was racing to comprehend as he described in his nutshell version what had happened. He was trying to keep me from worrying and at the same time attempting to prepare me for what I would see when I got home. He said that the fire truck had already left and was telling me that Mike was bringing Cara over to me when a tap sounded at the door, and there they were.

I hung up the phone to answer the door and hug my daughter who crumpled in my arms in tears, still not fully grasping everything that had transpired. I would not understand the full significance of what I'd been told until a while later, when I saw it for myself. I am so thankful that Nowlin sent Cara to me. He knew I would be worried if I couldn't see her with my own eyes.

The events of that day were traumatic, especially for Cara and Nowlin. I can't imagine how much worse it must have been for them. The rest of us didn't actually experience the burning of the house. We only saw the devastation in the aftermath.

Nothing Nowlin had said on the phone prepared me for the stark reality of the charred remains I encountered back at home. I made my way through the smoky wetness of the living room, past the drooping soggy Christmas tree, to get to the worst of the damage on the east end of the house.

I stopped short inside the door frame where blackened half-burnt wooden beams had fallen into an ashy wasteland that hours before had been our bedroom. Blue sky shone through, framed with slanted charcoal slats, and an eerie glint of sunshine radiated through the gaping walls, falling on the smoky mist like glitter hung in the air.

I stepped to the open window and peered out upon a mountain of water-soaked half-charred books and other items the firemen had tossed out as they cleared the shelf of anything that would burn.

A sickening knot twisted and grew in my stomach as I turned to see the empty closet. Nothing was left of our entire wardrobe but a few half-melted metal hangers and the clothes on our backs.

I sleepwalked down the dim back hallway as if in a nightmare from which I couldn't wake up. I passed the bathroom where the melting heat had caused the once aqua paint to singe brown and bubble on the wall adjacent to our bedroom. The soot clung so thickly to the enamel paint on the opposite wall I could have scrawled an S.O.S. message with my fingertip. I noted the disfigured shampoo bottles and the deformed contact lens case on the blackened countertop next to the sink, then continued to Cara's room.

Her unmade bed covers and curtains were gray with the dank heavy smoke that still lingered everywhere. The thought of Cara asleep in that same bed only a short while earlier brought me to my knees with thanksgiving.

For the next 30 minutes, we gathered the kids' clothes and some bedding from the linen closet that we could wash and use over the course of the next few days. We cleared out the food from the refrigerator to take with us to Mike's, where we would stay until we could collect ourselves enough to know what to do next.

While we were still in the house, we noticed the smoke seemed to be getting thicker again, and traced it back to our bedroom where we spotted a wooden stud in the wall that was still smoldering. Nowlin raced to get the garden hose while I called the fire department again.

Coughing from the smoke, we cleared the way for the firemen to get back into the bedroom and vacated to the yard. Once the firemen were sure the fire was really out this time, we piled our few possessions into the minivan and left our beloved home, exhausted and sick with the realization that our life as we knew it had changed forever.

In the hours, days, and months after the fire, God continued to reveal to us the many ways in which his purpose was at work that day, his hand guiding us and his angels protecting us.

I don't know how He managed to stall Mike—probably Bret lingering too long over warm cinnamon rolls and milk while likely getting an earful from Mike about them being so late—but in Mike's tardiness that morning, so out of character for him, God's timing was perfect.

If he'd been on time as usual, Nowlin would already have left, and Cara would have been home alone, sleeping, in a burning house. I still can't bring myself to follow that thought to its end. It's too horrifying, too unthinkable.

If the plastic bags hadn't fed the blaze so quickly after the faulty wall plug ignited, Nowlin might have been injured trying to put the flames out by himself.

If Smokey hadn't run back into the burning house, Nowlin wouldn't have bothered to close the hall door containing the worst of the damage to one end of the building. If that door had been left open, the fire would have spread much more quickly, according to the firemen, and the entire structure would have burned to the ground and been a total loss.

Fortunately, most of the house, though water logged and smoke damaged, was salvaged. We were able to sell it "as is" to a restoration and remodeling company for enough money to help pay cash, when added to the insurance money, for a bigger, newer home in the same neighborhood where the kids were already going to school, thus ending the long treks back and forth across town.

I will praise God forever for His grace and mercy, protection and loving kindness toward us that day. The fullness of His perfect timing, power, and protective vigilance continued to reveal itself to us in the months that followed, the enormity of which I cannot begin to recount here. Eternal echoes of unexplainable details, and salvation from the horrors of "What if?!" began to change us individually, and collectively, as a family.

It was the day a new kind of flame was kindled, the steady sure blaze of tested faith. Faith tried by fire but not consumed with the stubble. It would never be extinguished, only fanned by other trials to even greater heights.

# A Father's Answer

In spite of decades of teaching and with Brian preparing to go off to college in the fall of 2000, it was hard to realize the impact of so much time passing and of how old my parents were. It had been a wakeup call when Mom had her heart attack, and the events around the house fire made it crystal clear that anything can happen and that life is sometimes changed forever in a single moment.

Even when we finally stop to see that others around us are growing older, we seldom recognize as readily how we ourselves have changed. It's a stark realization when we see that we *are* the "older generation" and that the elders who have cared for us, if we're blessed to still have them among us, now need our care and attention.

As unprepared and kiddish as we feel inside, the torch has been passed to us. How in the world will we carry it? I'm sure our parents felt the same way, and we'll handle it exactly as they did, with the help and by the grace of God, one day at a time. We'll pass the wisdom we've gained from our mistakes to our children and pray they listen so they won't have to make the same ones themselves. We'll look at the errors of our parents, knowing the consequences we suffered, and strive to do things a little better for our own children.

It's the nature of life in this world: decades of searching, sometimes by trial and error, for what is good and right. For love, true joy, and peace of mind. Searching for a way to live *in* this world but not be *of* it.

In the end, when we're less distracted by the world itself and when we're better able to learn it, we find the simple truth that all those good things we longed for are found in one place: in God Himself. We realize that all along He has been expressing Himself, revealing Himself in the loving relationships and through the circumstances around us. Our wise Father uses it all—the good and bad, the beautiful and sometimes the very ugly—to draw us step-by-step, year-by-year closer to Him. Ironically, He often uses death to teach us about life—real life, eternal life with Him.

One of my favorite scriptures is Romans 8:28, "And we know that all things work together for good to those who love God, to those who are the called according to His purpose." Those comforting words have sustained me in many difficult seasons of hardship and loss. I've seen their truth borne out in countless circumstances in my own life.

I've been tempted to look back at some dark and painful periods and say, "Why, Lord, did I have to go through that?" or "How could I not see the mistake I was making?" But the Spirit has brought that verse to mind and shown me, more clearly every time, that in spite of my limited knowledge, my misinformation, or lack of understanding—and no matter how devious and deadly the schemes of the evil one to throw me off track, derail my purpose, and render me useless—God has always been faithful to turn those things around which were meant for evil and work them for my good instead.

I can now agree with the apostle Paul, "Being confident of this very thing, that he who has begun a good work in you [me] will complete it until the day of Jesus Christ..." (Philippians 1:6). From the moment He prayed for me and for all future believers 2,000 years ago, Jesus has always had my back. He's always been my best friend, even long before I knew Him.

The months surrounding my father's death were no exception. In fact, looking back, God revealed Himself in amazing ways to many in my family amid and through the painful circumstances of Dad's passing. He poured out His peace and strength, and in those poignant, intimate moments with eternity, He let us glimpse the height, breadth, and depth of His love for each one of his children.

After many healthy years of doting on grandchildren and enjoying the work and the solitude of his vegetable garden, Dad was diagnosed with Parkinson's disease, which had many challenges. He dealt with them quietly and gracefully for most of a decade before his doctors discovered he also had lung cancer in the fall of 1999.

Because of the prolonged battle with Parkinson's and the related medicines he had been on to slow its effects, Dad wasn't a candidate for invasive surgery to remove the cancer, even though tests showed it was concentrated in one small area about the size of a quarter. The only viable treatment option was radiation. At first, Dad sustained the series of targeted radiation treatments fairly well for his 81 years. Late in the following spring, however, his health began to decline rather quickly, so Dubie and I would take turns at night staying with Mom and Dad in their home in Broken Arrow.

Even though the ultimate demise of our beloved "Daddy" was a sad premise, those last few months of Dad's life were, even at the time, a sweet and precious gift from God, riddled with heavenly encounters and glimpses of another life and realm, overflowing with God's love and presence.

Like the times when Dad would get up at night to go to the bathroom and, being always unsteady and off balance from the Parkinson's disease, would almost lose his footing and fall but for the steadying hand that stabilized him, by his own account, more than once. He told my sister of one time in particular when he turned to thank Mom for her help. He felt a strong, gentle hand on his elbow that had kept him from going to the floor when his feet wouldn't move. Regaining his balance, he turned to express his appreciation only to find that she was sound asleep on the other side of the bed, facing the opposite direction!

Then there was an evening on Dubie's watch when Dad lowered the newspaper he was reading to ask her in an oh-by-the-way sort of question, "Who was that young man at the table with us at lunch today?" My sister was taken off guard and didn't know quite how to respond.

She indicated that she didn't understand what he meant and reminded him that there had only been Mother and she at the table with him. He looked at my sister incredulously, and very exasperated, he insisted somewhat condescendingly, "Well, I *know* you and your mother! But who was the young man sitting next to me?" To that, she could only reply, truthfully, "I don't know, Dad. I really don't know who it was."

When Dubie told me about the incident later, how matter-of-fact his question had been, and his exasperation at her noncomprehension of such a simple inquiry, we came to the same conclusion, that perhaps Dad *had* actually seen someone. Someone very real, but that she couldn't see.

Another time I sat down beside Dad after breakfast, thinking how I would broach the subject that he should drink more water. The nurse had said that to keep the toxins from building up in his system we had to find a way to get more water down him, to flush them out. We would leave a glass of water on the table by his chair, but often hours went by with no more than a few sips taken.

I didn't want to nag. Dad was always such a thinking man, surely I could appeal to his reasoning and get him to understand how critically important it was to keep his body well hydrated. I patted his leg and began, "Dad, there's something really important I need to talk to you about..."

As I paused to form the next words, only for a split second, he covered my hand with his, patting it. With the sweetest, most celestial smile, he nodded his head and said, "I know: Jesus Christ." I was flabbergasted! Much as I love the Lord, He was far from the subject of my thoughts in that particular moment. Apparently, though, He was very near to Dad's and very much on his mind.

The most amazing incident, however, at least from my perspective, happened near the end, just a day or two before he died. By this time, Mom and Dad had moved in with Dubie and Oman, early in July. Oman had remodeled part of their house into a suite for our parents where they could still have some privacy and their own space, yet be close to immediate help when needed.

For a month or so Dad held his own, with a mix of good days and bad. The first week in August, however, he took a turn for the worse. We were all vigilant about being there, wanting to spend as much time as we could with Dad in those brief moments of consciousness. As his pain grew worse and the morphine level was increased, he slipped into longer and longer periods of comatose sleep, only rousing occasionally with a moan of pain.

The family was all around. While Dad was resting, we would visit, or several of us would sit down to pray together. Sometimes, we would each be lost in our own silent thoughts and prayers. We all knew we were just waiting for the inevitable.

One afternoon, Mom, Dubie, Karen, and I were all in Dad's room together. The three of them were talking quietly in the sitting area at one end of the large suite. I was seated about halfway up the adjacent wall, closer to the side of the room where Dad's bed was. I was silently reading my Bible, soaking in all the passages that have been especially uplifting and comforting to me during many other difficult times. Dad had not been awake to speak or move on his own for a couple of days.

Suddenly, he stretched his arm out, and calling me by name, he said, "Diana, come here." I was startled and excited that he was awake. I dragged my chair quickly to his bedside to hear what he was going to say, praying that I wouldn't miss a word of it.

With a broad sweeping gesture of his left arm, he described, in a clearer voice than I had heard in many days, what he saw, "It's like a paintbrush, a rainbow of colors, beautiful, brilliant colors…" The stroking motion of his arm stopped, and he brought it back to his side. Still staring, as if through the wall at something else, he added in a quiet but very distinct voice, "I see five angels."

I wanted to hear more. I asked him what else he saw. but when I looked at him, his eyes were closed again. He had resumed the shallow, irregular breathing of his coma-like state. Those were the last intelligible words he spoke, to my knowledge.

I was euphoric as I repeated the message to the others in the room, who had witnessed the exchange but hadn't heard as clearly as I had. We knew that Dad had described to us a heavenly scene that he was experiencing as God prepared to take him home. We knew what a rare and sacred privilege it was for us to have the eye-witness account of someone who was on the threshold of stepping into the heavenly life.

We were enthralled and basking in the love and comfort that God had so miraculously showered upon us. As we marveled at the encounter and repeated the events for those who were not present in the room, the question occurred to me, *"Why me?"* Why had Dad called my name?

I knew it wasn't that he loved me any more than my sisters. Mom had been his sweetheart and "bride" for 57 years. Why had God chosen me to receive and relate that heavenly message? My sisters and mother were no less spiritual, no lesser women of faith than I. Why me? It was a mystery I couldn't explain. It was one more demonstration of God's inexplicable grace—unmerited, undeserved, and unearned favor.

It was only in the weeks and months after Dad's passing, when I was meditating on the things that had transpired, that the Spirit very matter-of-factly, in one of those eye-opening 'duh' moments, reminded me that it was I who, as a young child, had asked my Daddy so earnestly about what heaven would be like. He hadn't had an answer then. It was only logical and fitting, however, that when Dad finally had an answer to that 40-something-year-old question, he would direct that response, in his last hours here on earth, to me.

I can look back on those horrible episodes of fear I experienced most of my young life and from the vantage point of time passed, see God's tender hand holding and molding me. Shaping me into something truly new. In retrospect, many of the subsequent difficulties which perhaps should have been more consequential and heavy to bear didn't seem so because God had already used that first real trial to draw me close and leave me no choice but to trust Him so that He could prove Himself present and faithful in all the rest.

It still overwhelms me and brings tears of joy when I think of those events and the marvelous way in which God works *all* things for good, even the dark and scary periods, to answer questions, to teach us things, and ultimately, to draw us to a deeper understanding and a more glorious experience of Him.

He is with us, each one individually, when we come face-to-face with our demons. When we finally reach the end of ourselves and realize how completely unable and utterly helpless we are to overcome them on our own, there is Jesus. With loving arms wide open, He's saying "I know you can't. But I can. Trust Me. Lean on Me. Rest in Me. I've already done it for you."

Glory to God, I now have an answer when my grandchildren ask me to tell them about heaven, not based on supposition but on an eye-witness report that both my heavenly Father and my earthly Daddy loved me enough to bring me.

GODSWAY

# Divine Reassurance

One thing I know to be true about the humanity of teachers is that they remember the problem child better than any of their other pupils. The average students—well-behaved, intelligent, quiet, and respectful (yes, they *are* the majority!)— are lost to oblivion with the passing of years. Thankfully, God knows every one of them by name and has not forgotten them.

For the teacher, those who cause the least disturbance and need the least help are, ironically, the ones that most often slip through the mesh of memory because the teacher intuitively knows they'll be okay. They're going to make it, with or without help. The teacher loves them, enjoys them, and thanks God for the order and sanity they bring to the classroom. Those foundational students, who comprise the backbone of the educational system, come and go, often without being noticed.

Mixed in with these students every year, however, are those few individuals whose domestic circumstances so reflect the ills of our society or just the hard-knock life of this world, that they come to school with a host of problems. Their challenges and deficiencies range from behavioral and emotional to social and academic in all the combinations thereof. They always struggle at something.

Those are the students that the heart of a true teacher anguishes over because the teacher knows it's not just about academics; it's about the whole child. They're the strugglers for whom the teacher spends countless hours in meetings, in planning—and in prayer—to find a way to "get through" and give them what they truly need. They're the defiants who challenge authority, try patience to the limit, and cause teachers to question their ability and their very calling. These children are the faces imprinted timelessly on the screen of teachers' memories. They're the lost sheep that the shepherd leaves the 99 to search for.

There have been many such students in my 30-something years of teaching. What joy and satisfaction it brings when they come back to visit years later or when I encounter them in some aspect of their adult life and see that they did make it, after all! Once in a while, however, those later encounters are not reassuring but in fact, a source of greater worry and anxiety than ever. So it was with Rafael.

Rafael Navarro came to me in one of the years that our English as a Second Language Center was split up into satellite locations. The ESL enrollment was experiencing such unprecedented growth that it became difficult to find an existing school in the district whose building had enough empty space to house the entire ESL Center in one location.

Thus, for a few years we were separated though still under the same parent program. I was at the MacArthur Elementary satellite with one other ESL teacher. She taught the primary grades, and I taught the upper elementary grades, which meant the classes were combined grade levels.

We had the children for about five hours a day, during which time we focused mainly on English vocabulary and language skills (listening, speaking, reading and writing) while also trying to incorporate as much of the grade-level content curriculum as possible. Given the students' varying backgrounds as to availability of educational opportunities in their home country, and their families' differing abilities to access them, they were at all levels in every subject area. Further, in a program that served immigrant families from all over the world who were new to the Tulsa area, the economic hardships and emotional anxieties of having left friends, relatives, language, and culture behind were givens among the population. Teaching to that wide range of needs was a monumental task. The logistics of the service we provided, from both the district's financial and geographical perspective, dictated that the same teacher would have some students two or more years in a row, long before "looping" came into vogue.

Rafael came to me as a 4th grader. His mother had died in Mexico after his father had already abandoned them, and he had recently come here to live with an aunt. Sympathetic as I was to his situation, it was so similar to many others that he didn't stand out at first. He was quiet, even-tempered, and seemed eager to please, though academically, even aside from the English language issue, he was way behind for his age. With a sketchy school attendance record in Mexico, he had not fully grasped the fundamentals of reading in his native Spanish, thus there were few skills that he could transfer to the learning of a second language. He struggled from the beginning. Most new students had difficulties for a while, but with time those who had sound educational backgrounds in their native countries and strong family support made the emotional and cultural adjustments, and the academics began to fall into place.

I am not a trained psychologist and would not begin to venture a diagnosis of Rafael's problems. However, in retrospect, it seems logical that he must have suffered from feelings of abandonment, grief, and displacement, all of which exacerbated the already difficult task of attending school in a foreign language and culture. Well into the first year, things were still not connecting for him. With no stable adult male role models, he struggled in forming friendships and constantly strove to find ways to fit in with the other students, especially with the boys. As he fell further behind academically, he tried harder than ever to find acceptance in other ways: the usual talking, joking, silly antics to draw a laugh, always pretending he didn't take anything seriously.

He was with me a second year in 5th grade, and we had a few breakthroughs. He was starting to make some real progress in oral language, vocabulary, and basic math. Emotionally and socially, however, he was still battling the unseen darkness. A couple of the new fifth-graders befriended him at first. He tried to play soccer with them at recess, but he wasn't very good at it.

On one occasion when his team finally won, the boys were ecstatic with celebration. Having never learned the social boundaries, however, of accepted physical contact with other males, Rafael made the huge faux pas of hugging one of the other boys a little too tightly and a little too long. It would seem like nothing today, but the reaction back then was immediate and unmistakable, " Huy, vete, maricón! No hagas eso! No me toques más!" The equivalent of "Hey, sissy [or 'queer,' 'fag,' 'gay,' whichever hateful label fits your generation's lingo] get away from me! Don't do that! Don't touch me again!"

Some horrible seeds were planted that day, and my heart broke for Rafael. For the rest of the year, he was an outcast among the boys. Consequently, he tried all the more to fit in with the girls, choosing to spend his recesses and free time doing things he knew they liked to do, such as drawing, coloring, jumping rope, and picking flowers, just to have a sense of belonging somewhere. By the end of the year, the cruel stereotype was in place. He was still behind, fighting to catch up with the ever-growing curriculum demands, and now had fallen into behavior patterns that I knew would cause him even bigger problems in middle school.

A group of other teachers, administrators, and I made the decision to retain him in 5th grade the following year, hoping the extra time in elementary school would give him a chance to build a firmer foundation in reading and math, as well as to mature emotionally, before he had to face the stringent demands of 6th grade.

Inwardly, I felt it would be best to separate him from this group of students with whom he had a history and a reputation, to give him a chance to start with a clean slate in the fall. Little did I know, in my naïveté, that Rafael himself was either beginning to believe the lies of the stereotype or at least was going along with it as the only way to find the attention and affection he craved.

Unfortunately, I fear the extra year did little more than put off the inevitable as he continued to cast himself in the same role even with the new group. Although his academic foundation was somewhat stronger, nothing really changed that last year—except his voice.

He was headed to Whitney Middle School still fighting a losing battle to bridge the academic gap, still desperately trying to fit in socially somehow with someone, and now dealing with the scary, confusing onset of puberty.

I sent him on to 6th grade genuinely concerned for his physical safety as much as for his academic progress and profoundly burdened for his emotional and spiritual welfare. I prayed for him often, and for a year or so, he came by my room from time to time to say hi after school since Whitney was right next to MacArthur in the same city block. He was always friendly and I took heart that he seemed to be adjusting and doing alright.

On one afternoon visit, he was particularly excited about his upcoming birthday party. While I was finishing my preparations for the next day and gathering up what I needed to take home for the evening, Rafael was bubbling about the who, where, and when of his big celebration. He invited me to come. Knowing I wouldn't remember otherwise, I wrote down the date, time, and address, and tucked the note in my pocket, thinking it would be good for me to attend.

However, Nowlin was a commercial driver now and was away from home much of the time. He'd gone to driving school and was hauling loads in an 18-wheel truck to help with finances and try to get ahead of the kids' college expenses. He was on the road so much of the time that the weekends when he was home were like a different life for me. It was rare time, our time, to spend together, catching up on news and family events and then getting ready for him to leave for his next delivery.

By the time I found the slip of paper again, the date of Rafael's party had already passed. I felt guilty for having missed it. I knew that I was one of the few people Rafael counted on, and I had let him down.

I felt terrible and apologized profusely the next time I saw him. I'm very sure the apology didn't make up for the missed opportunity, though he readily forgave me. He acted like it was okay though I knew it hurt and disappointed him more than he let on. He didn't come by much after that.

A year or two later, the ESL program moved again, into the Walter Reed Elementary building where all the classes would be together again and later become the fully accredited Newcomer International School. I lost contact with Rafael and became absorbed in current issues and problems.

There were new students to serve, new mandates to meet from NCLB (No Child Left Behind), and mounting pressure to improve state test scores. Yes, even among a constantly fluctuating population of newly arrived English learners, the higher powers—I'm not talking spiritual here—were more interested in tests scores than what was truly best for these students. I was frustrated with the situation and busier than ever. I'll be honest, I seldom thought of Rafael.

In the spring of 2002, after a Friday evening Easter Tenebrae service at our church, in which my family participated, we stopped at a Tex-Mex restaurant for dinner. We had invited a couple of friends to attend the service, so the group was larger than usual. We didn't have reservations, but the staff was accommodating and pushed some tables together in order to seat us all next to each other.

We settled in, perusing the menus when a hesitant voice from behind me inquired, "Mrs. Keathley?" Surprised at hearing my name, I turned around and found myself face-to-face with the new busboy, Rafael! We were elated to see each other.

The voice was deeper, but the same wide grin spread across the now peach-fuzz-covered jaws and chin. I couldn't believe he was old enough to have a job! He explained that at 15½ years old, he was allowed to work a few hours per week, in the early evenings, on busy nights, to earn a little money although, he was not allowed to wait tables, serve food, or run the cash register yet.

During the course of our meal that night Rafael came by several times to visit for a minute or two before scurrying off to clean up a vacated table or booth. When we got ready to leave, I stood up and looked around for him. He must have been watching as he appeared out of nowhere to give me a big hug and a stuffed animal out of the vending machine in the foyer. We exchanged phone numbers and addresses to keep in touch. This time, I intended to do just that.

I wrote Rafael a letter a short while after we'd first seen him at the restaurant. I knew he didn't have time for long conversations while he was at work, so I thought we could catch up on the missing years in letters. I certainly didn't want to drop the ball again as I'd done with the birthday party.

I think I got a letter back from him, too. For the next several months, when Nowlin would come home exhausted from his latest stint on the road, he and I would go out for a bite to eat, and to chill at our favorite destination as much for Rafael's presence as for the great food.

Once Rafael knew we were there, he would come by the table several times to exchange news, or ask about the family or about something he remembered from the ESL days. He'd stop for a minute or two at a time and then move on so as not to get caught wasting time on the clock.

One evening, however, he loitered at our table more than usual but didn't say much. It struck me as odd at the time, and I tried to make conversation, asking him about his plans for the summer and the following school year.

Finally, he actually sat down in the booth with us and said that he didn't really like school and was thinking about quitting and moving in with a friend. I tried not to react too harshly but was sure it was not what he needed to do. I asked him what his aunt thought about it, and he said his aunt wouldn't let him stay with her any more. She didn't like his friend.

I protested that Rafael and his friend weren't old enough to rent an apartment and be on their own. He responded, "My friend is. He's 23. My aunt doesn't like him because...you know, because he's a boy." He was looking at me expectantly, to see my reaction.

The realization of what he was telling me hit me like a ton of bricks though it shouldn't have. I don't remember how I recovered or exactly what I said except in general terms that he should not make any hasty decisions. He should try to work things out to stay at home with his aunt and definitely to stay in school.

I went home from that encounter horrified that some 23-year-old man was taking advantage of Rafael's youth, confusion, and emotional needs. I wrote him another letter, one that was much more direct than I was comfortable with, but I knew I had to. I felt his future and perhaps his life style were being usurped by someone else, not allowing Rafael to discover for himself who he really was.

I warned him that there were people who would seem to care about him, but who would really only take advantage of him, and that in spite of his feelings, he was much too young to be involved in *any kind* of sexual relationship. I begged him not to move in with the man but to stay in school and give himself time to grow and mature and to figure things out for himself.

I urged him to find a church and seek God. I told him how much God loved him and that He knew everything Rafael was thinking and feeling— all the hurt and loneliness of his young life. I don't remember word for word what I wrote in that letter. I only know I was desperate to turn him away from that older man and into the arms of God.

I prayed over the writing of the letter and prayed when I mailed it that God would prepare Rafael's heart for its truth. I prayed that God would intervene and spare him from being lured into a wrong and damaging relationship while still a minor with someone eight years his senior. I believed the other man was clearly and knowingly taking advantage of Rafael's vulnerability. I prayed that this already fragile teenage boy, who was so close to my heart and who had already been through *so much,* would not be robbed of the opportunity to grow and learn for himself who Rafael really is.

I prayed constantly for days, my heart in my stomach. The scriptural phrase "pray without ceasing" took hold again as it had in the weeks before Cara was born. At every pause in my routine, every quiet moment between lessons, and even between responses in the "wait time" so necessary to English learners, my thoughts and my very heart were filled with anguish and desperate pleas for Rafael. It was the most helpless feeling I'd ever had concerning any student—ever.

*"I went before God, Diana, to carry him."* In the wee hours of Wednesday morning, May 15, 2002, a male-sounding voice woke me from a deep sleep with the above statement. Someone had spoken to me, and it woke me up.

I looked around the empty bedroom trying to make sense of it. Then, I heard the voice again, delivering the same message a second time to my consciousness. *"I went before God, Diana, to carry him."* It was a gentle, deliberate, and precise utterance.

At first, I didn't understand the message or the messenger. The words were clear, and the voice had called me by name. What did it mean? It was not a voice that spoke in time and space. I heard it from inside, yet it was unmistakable. I knew it was significant, a communication specifically for me, from another realm. So, I switched on the light, fumbled for a pen, and grabbed a notebook from the desk nearby to write down the exact sentence, word for word. I turned the light off and lay down in bed again, still not fully understanding the celestial event.

Musing, I knew it must be from God. That perfect voice, familiar, warm, full of authority and love, had pronounced my name intimately, without hesitation, as if he'd known me from the foundations of the earth.

So, who needed to be carried? I pondered the question, wondering if Nowlin, who was out on the road at the time, was in some kind of predicament. Then, I remembered whom I'd been praying for non-stop for 5-6 days. Every time I would wake in the night, at every pause in my day, God would bring Rafael back to my mind, and I would pray all over again.

Now I knew the meaning of that glorious heavenly message! Rafael would be fine. God was assuring me that Rafael was safe in His loving hands, a lost sheep found and carried to safety. My heart was flooded with relief and "joy unspeakable and full of glory."

I haven't seen Rafael since the divine reassurance of that early May morning in 2002. When I think of that problem child with the wide grin and sweet spirit, I wonder sometimes where he is and what he is doing, but I don't ever worry. If God will send a messenger directly to me, just to relieve *my* anguish over my former student, imagine what He will do for Rafael himself, exceeding abundantly above all that I ask or think!

GODSWAY

# Small Details,
# Exponential Impact

Everyone experiences little coincidences. When they occur, we pause momentarily and think "How odd!" and then quickly pass the incident off instead of truly pondering its significance. However, we should learn to recognize God's fingerprints in those odd little moments just as much as in the blatant miracles.

His handiwork is seen not just in the majesty of snow-covered mountain peaks and the million breathtaking shades of autumn leaves but also in the unique design of a single leaf's veins and in the delicate and detailed embryo hidden inside the acorn. God is just as much glorified by the infinitesimally tiny as by the cosmically huge.

When we learn to see God's hand at work even in the seemingly insignificant details of our lives, He is eager to show us more and more of Himself as we trust Him with more and as we seek to know Him better. How else can I explain the fact that the first time I actually thought to buckle my toddler Bret into a seatbelt in the back seat before it was the law would be the day he opened the car door at full speed on the highway?

How else can I reconcile that during a span of about a month when I was having a recurring dream about a house fire, it came to my attention that through an error at the mortgage company our house insurance had lapsed so I called and had it reinstated? And that after buying and leaving smoke detectors in a drawer uninstalled for more than six months, Nowlin finally put them up within weeks before we actually did have a house fire? How else can I interpret the fact that during the fire, every thread of clothing that was hanging in my closet was incinerated off the hangers into nothingness, a gaping hole in the wall showed blue sky where the fire had burned all the way through, and plywood musical cases were disintegrated from around instruments, yet the instruments themselves, some wooden guitars, were for the most part unscathed? How is it possible that of a plastic notebook filled with hundreds of original songs, poems, and other writings, hand-written on sheets of paper, sitting in the same burning bedroom, *not one page of original work was lost?*

Friends, these are not coincidences. These are God's way of getting our attention to show us how close He really is. He wants us to trust Him, and the more we understand His continual presence and the depth of His love, the easier it gets to trust Him with all things, large and small.

One time at the ESL Center, in the early years when we were still at Byrd, I had taken my class outside for recess. It was fun to watch children from a dozen countries around the globe run and play together, communicating with gestures and their limited English. At the end of recess, I had successfully corralled most of the large group to go inside. The stragglers were Florianne, a little French girl, and Kai, from Korea, who had struck up an unlikely friendship while gathering flowers. Kai ran past me at the sound of the whistle and followed the rest of the group inside behind the other teacher, but Florianne stopped short. She looked at me with distressed eyes. Although she couldn't verbalize in English what the problem was, I quickly understood from her gestures that something was wrong with her foot. She pointed to one sandal and then to the other and shrugged her shoulders glancing around the playground. Then, I noticed that one sandal was missing its decorative bow.

I realized in an instant it would be like finding a needle in a haystack since she and Kai had wandered over most of the acre-plus field gathering dandelions and other flowering weeds. I knew we couldn't spend much time looking for the bow, so I silently asked for some help, *"Lord, help us find it. You know exactly where it is. Show us where to look."*

Florianne and I split up and started searching. My eyes were quickly scanning broad stretches of the ground as I walked. Spying nothing after a few seconds but still praying, I turned to look in another direction. There, precisely at the tip of my toe, was the missing bow that I'd almost stepped on. I grabbed it up and hollered that I'd found it.

I thanked God silently, and as we walked inside together I shared with Florianne that I had prayed and God answered my prayer. In that teachable moment, I added that we can always go to God for what we need, even the little things.

Another incident occurred a year or two after the house fire. I was getting ready for bed one night in our still-new-to-us home and discovered when I started to take my earrings out that one of my opals was missing. I frantically combed through the multicolored carpet in the dressing area hoping I had just lost it and it would still be lying there on top, blending in with the other dots of color—to no avail.

I searched through every square inch of both drawers of the vanity thinking if they were opened slightly, it could have fallen inside. Not there. I poured over every stitch of clothing I'd had on, thinking the earring might have gotten caught in the fabric as I was changing clothes, but still nothing.

I was heartsick. I mentally retraced my day and realized I could have lost the opal earring in any one of a dozen different places. I had no idea when or where it had fallen from my ear. I was never one for a lot of expensive jewelry, but these earrings were special. The opals were my October birthstone and the earrings a gift from Nowlin to replace a set I'd lost in the fire. The sentimental value was as great as the monetary.

For the next couple of days, I looked in every place I knew I had been the day the earring went missing, scanning the floors and furniture, always with an eye searching, even while going about daily tasks, hoping by some miracle to find it.

After several days of unanswered prayers and futile searching, I resigned myself to the fact that it was gone for good and gave up the hunt with one final prayer. *"Lord, I know it's only a worldly possession. I shouldn't be so attached to something with no real eternal value. I can live without it. But I know You know where it is. If possible, according to Your will, in Your own time, bring the opal back to me for Nowlin's sake as much as mine."*

Life went on. I'm not sure how much time passed—at least a couple of weeks, probably more—long enough that I'd stopped thinking about and lamenting over the lost opal. I'd moved on.

Then, one morning the alarm went off, and I flipped on the light to start my pre-dawn routine of getting ready for work. I zipped on my robe, and when my eyes had adjusted, I moved toward the bedroom door to go downstairs and start the much needed morning coffee, but a sparkle from the sink caught my eye as I was turning around. I stepped back to see the source, and there, framed against the white porcelain, sitting pretty-as-a-picture in the middle of the sink bowl, was my opal earring.

I couldn't believe my eyes. I had used that sink dozens of times since the earring had been lost. It absolutely had not been there before. I'd searched the countertop, the drawers, the carpet, and yes, the sink, over and over. It had been nowhere in sight, for more than two weeks.

And now, there it was, winking at me. Not caught in the drain, not to the side, or half hidden under something, but squarely in the middle of the sink bowl – in full and obvious view – where it could not have been before. What a delightful and playful flare for the dramatic our Creator has!

Several years later there was another extraordinary happening which occurred when I was in a rush for work. That of itself was not unusual. It seemed like no matter how early I got up, I found extra things to do and always wound up hurrying at the last minute.

This day was only different in that I hadn't brought home the usual bags of papers the night before, so the morning exit simply entailed grabbing my purse. I locked and pulled the front door closed behind me until I heard the click, then twisted the knob and pushed to make sure it was locked.

I had formed that habit when it came to my attention that one of Bret's friends never closed the door all the way. Often when James left the house, he only half-heartedly closed the door, not pulling it behind him until the latch clicked. I would find a short time later that the door had come slightly ajar. Because of that, I was always careful to listen for the click and then twist the door knob to make sure it was actually locked.

Confident the house was secure, I scampered down the steps toward the van, digging in my purse for the familiar key ring enroute. At the van door, I was still rummaging for the illusive keys, now searching carefully through every compartment of the large handbag.

When my fingers came up empty again, I realized I must have locked them inside the house. What would I do? There was no one home to let me in. Mike, who had lived on the same side of town while we were on 4th Street, had moved to a house right behind us a few years after the house fire. I remembered that we had given our new backyard neighbor a spare house key for just such emergencies. I would simply walk around and borrow it.

Then, it dawned on me, I was running so late that Mike, always an early bird—well, except on one notable occasion—was already at work. I hated to bother him and ask him to make an extra trip home, but what else could I do? The kids were all away at college by now, and Nowlin was on the road. At least, Mike was working only half time these days, and his hours were flexible. He could make them up later in the week if he didn't want to go all the way back to the office again.

I reached for my relatively new flip phone, hoping I had Mike's work number and thinking I needed to call the secretary at school too to let them know I'd be a little late. Where was my phone? Then, I remembered I had plugged it in to recharge while I was getting ready for school, still not firmly in the habit of charging it ahead of time.

I walked back to the porch, tried the door handle again, and then sat down on the bench to think, pray, and search my purse one last time. When it was clear that neither the keys nor the phone were in my bag, I asked God to please help me, show me what to do.

I couldn't call Mike or the school without my cell phone. I couldn't drive to a pay phone without my keys. Before long, the 4th graders in the Spanish Immersion school where I was now teaching would be waiting unattended at my locked classroom. If I walked to a pay phone to call a cab I would be so late my principal and colleagues would be very worried.

I glanced at the closed front door and the van, asking myself why I had to be so sure everything was always locked up? *How could I be so stupid to not have my keys or phone with me?!* I was frustrated at myself but tried to see the humor in it.

I looked around the neighborhood at the quiet houses and empty driveways. I thought, *"Well Lord, thank you that this is not a life-and-death kind of emergency. I'll just start knocking on doors, and please let someone be home so I can use their telephone."* I had turned to walk down the steps, still asking God to work it out quickly so my students wouldn't be left alone in the hallway and people wouldn't be worried about me.

As I reached the bottom step, still not believing I was going to have to go door-to-door for help, something told me to turn around, to try the door handle one more time. I knew it was useless. I *knew* the door was locked. I'd heard the click. I'd twisted the knob and pushed to be sure. I had even tried it *again* after I realized I didn't have my keys, but I obeyed the voice that told me to check again.

As I turned around to walk back up the steps, I thought my eyes were playing tricks on me. I squinted and shaded them to be sure. The front door that I knew had been locked and that just a few seconds before had still been closed was now standing eight inches open.

Certainly not a James moment of inattention or half-hearted effort on my part, this was definitely a God moment! I raced inside to grab my things, laughing, shaking my head at His continued, wondrous accommodation in my times of need.

Sometimes, the details we trust Him with can make an exponential impact not just on our own lives but on others' as well. Most often, we don't get to know about the impact our faith and obedience have on others, as with Rafael. Once in a while, though, we're allowed to see face-to-face the impact we have on another's life and their faith when we "trust and obey."

One Saturday morning in the spring of 2015, I was dressing and curling my hair to run a few errands when I thought about the hospital. I felt a strange urge to go and visit someone, but I couldn't think of anyone I knew who was in the hospital at the time. I thought it was odd and tried to ignore it. I continued curling my hair.

In the weeks before, I'd been listening to a series from my church about being sensitive to the promptings of the Spirit. So, wanting to be sensitive but thinking of all the things I needed to do, I half-heartedly said, "Okay, Lord, I'm listening. What's this about?" I was feeling a distinct urge now to go to the children's hospital to encourage someone. I resisted, thinking maybe I'd go by there later while I was out running errands if I still felt lead to. Then, I heard the Spirit say plainly, *"Go now."*

In mid-curl, I asked the Lord, *"Right now, in the middle of hair curling and make-up?"* I remember questioning the Lord because it seemed so bizarre to stop with only half of my hair curled and go to the hospital to "encourage" someone, especially when I didn't even know who it was. As I questioned, the Spirit answered matter-of-factly, *"She'll be gone if you wait."* So, I quickly turned off the curling iron, grabbed my purse and keys, and went straight to the children's hospital just over a mile from my house.

I felt silly getting out of the car with half of my hair curled and half straight, but there was no mistaking the message I was getting from God. I knew it must be important. I was invested now, and as I approached the building, I was earnestly praying for guidance. I asked about which elevator to take, what floor, every step of the way, in order to find the person I was supposed to meet.

I was led to a small waiting area in the lobby of the infant surgery floor, near the elevator I'd just exited. There was a young Black woman with a couple of small children sitting quietly. A baby carriage was parked next to her chair, empty. Not knowing for sure if this was whom I was supposed to talk to, I sat down in an empty seat across from them.

After a minute or two, I asked the woman if this was the waiting room for families with children in surgery. She answered, "I'll take you down there." I followed her as she pushed the empty carriage down a nearby hallway. She stopped in front of a much larger waiting room and was about to open the door.

Sensing suddenly that she was the one I was sent to talk to, I asked her, "Do you have a child in surgery?" She nodded, "Yes. My son was born prematurely, and he's already had two surgeries. This will be his third."

I blurted out, "This is going to sound strange, but I feel I've been led to the hospital to encourage someone in the children's ward." I explained the sense of urgency God had impressed upon me to the point that I left home immediately, without finishing my curling job. "I feel silly with my hair half curled. I don't want you to think I'm some nut job, but I felt it was urgent. So, I followed what the Lord told me to do."

She watched me and listened intently as I explained my prompting. I asked if it would be alright if I prayed with her, and she readily said yes. I thanked the Lord for the precious family and the baby. I prayed for wisdom for the doctors who were operating on him and that the family would remember that God knows exactly what is wrong and how to fix it. And that He is able to do exceeding abundantly above all that we ask or think.

After the "...in Jesus' name, Amen," she thanked me with a rush of words she could hardly get out fast enough. She explained that she had just been praying and asking for help. She told God she needed some kind of positive sign, some encouragement to keep believing and hoping for the best. After describing her pleas to God, she added emphatically, "It's absolutely a miracle you showed up just at the precise moment when I needed that encouraging word!"

We visited for a few minutes, and I found out her name and her infant son's. I said I would keep praying for them and left, rather abruptly, it almost seemed. I barely remember the trip back home and had forgotten entirely about the errands I'd intended to run. I was almost giddy and a little breathless at having been a part of something so phenomenal, so important that God was doing in her and in me through that divine appointment. What a blessing!

I realized shortly afterward that we hadn't exchanged phone numbers. I didn't have any way to stay in touch, but I prayed for the woman and her son a lot for several weeks after the encounter. Now, when I think of them, I trust God that they are all doing well and that the baby is healthy and whole. I am at peace about it, like I am with Rafael.

Even though I haven't seen her since that day, I know this young mother was truly affected by the event. I remember the incredulous look on her face as I described the message and promptings I'd received from God. She was utterly astounded at the immediate way in which God had answered her prayer. The look on her face, her words, and her demeanor told me in the moment how much this event meant to her. Her faith and mine were bolstered that day. I know this is a story she'll tell her son one day as proof that God is good. He loves us, hears us, and sees us where we are. He uses the trivial things like hair curling—or *not* curling—to accomplish His mighty deeds.

In our faith journey, if we've been paying attention and have not dismissed God's promptings and His movement in the details of our circumstances as coincidence, we'll begin to understand that He *is* working in the little things that happen, to build us up. To get us ready.

As the small encounters mount up over time, we become persuaded that He is just as trustworthy when the huge scary trials come. And they do come. The tender thump and 3-word answer the night on the wall. The touch on my shoulder when I had no alarm clock in San Bernardino. The disappearing tire changer on a remote stretch of highway. All had prepared me to take the leap, to obey His command to "Let go!"

After I took that frightening plunge to obey His voice in the face of frenetic worldly circumstances on that highway, a lifetime of interacting with Him opened up, a lifetime of ever-expanding trust in Him and innumerable opportunities to witness his love and faithfulness in action, of a growing sense of awe at His power and might at work on my behalf, of deepening love for Him, and of genuine appreciation for His perpetual goodness. If we remind ourselves, when the profoundly scary crises descend upon us, that we already have a foundation laid in early snapshot moments when He showed up in small but extraordinary ways in the past, we know He is still right here with us, eager to help again and again and again. We're ready. Because we're *swayed* by and toward our great and loving God, with Whom all things are possible, we have GodSway.

GODSWAY

# Selected MSI Publications

*All MSI Press publications available on discount at www.msipress.com/ shop; use coupon code FF25 for 25% off any book.*

57 Steps to Paradise: Finding Love in Midlife and Beyond (Lorenz)

An Afternoon's Dictation (Greenebaum)

A Believer-in-Waiting's First Encounters with God (Mahlou)

A Guide to Bliss (Tubali)

A Theology for the Rest of Us (Yavelberg)

Blest Atheist (Mahlou)

Christmas at the Mission (Sula)

Día de Muertos (Sula)

Easter at the Mission (Sula)

El Poder de lo Transpersonal (Ustman)

Everybody's Little Book of Everyday Prayers (MacGregor)

God Speaks into Darkness (Easterling)

Good Blood (Schaffer)

Harnessing the Power of Grief (Potter)

Healing from Incest (Henderson & Emerton)

How to Argue with an Atheist (Brink)

Introductory Lectures on Religious Philosophy (Sabzevary)

Jesus Is Still Passing By: Secrets for a Victorious Life (Easterling)

Joshuanism (Tosto)

Lamentations of the Heart (Wells-Smith)

Learning to Feel (Girrell)

Life after Losing a Child (Young & Romer)

Life, Liberty, & Covid-19 (Ortman)

Living in Blue Sky Mind (Diedrichs)

Of God, Rattlesnakes, & Okra (Easterling )

One Family: Indivisible (Greenebaum)

Passing On (Romer)

Puertas a la Eternidad (Ustman)

Rainstorm of Tomorrow (Dong)

Saints I Know (Sula)

Seeking Balance in an Unbalanced Time (Greenebaum)

Since Sinai (Gonyou)

Sula and the Franciscan Sisters (Sula)

Surviving Cancer, Healing People: One Cat's Story (Sula)

Surviving Freshman Year (Jones)

Tale of a Mission Cat (Sula)

Typhoon Honey (Girrell & Sjogren)

Weekly Soul (Craigie)

When You're Shoved from the Right, Look to Your Left: Metaphors of Islamic Humanism (Omar Imady)